inked

Abingdon Press

NASHVILLE

Inked
Choosing God's Mark to Transform Your Life

This book is printed on acid-free paper.

Library of Congress Cataloging-in-Publication Data has been requested.

ISBN 978-1-4267-5118-9

13 14 15 16 17 18 19 20 21 22—10 9 8 7 6 5 4 3 2 1

MANUFACTURED IN THE UNITED STATES OF AMERICA

For Jimmy, Jordan, and Chasen. My heart is inked with more love for you than you know.
—KG

To my parents, Robert and LaVada Bostwick, who gave me a love of books.
To my husband, Gary, my mighty Warrior.
To our son Chris and his wife, Lindsay, and to our son Scott and Elise, for their love, encouragement and witness; and to our grandchildren Zachary, Jackson, and Regan, whose little lights shine and who hold the future—all inked by the King.
—JK

Contents

Words Become Flesh

The Word became flesh.

—John 1:14

Everybody's got a way of expressing their feelings, and mine is through tattoos.
—David Beckham

A tattoo can tell you a lot about a person. Some reflect a rebellious season, like the demons that cover Josh Hamilton of the Texas Rangers. Some express religious ties, like actor Mark Wahlberg's once tattooed rosary. Some are symbols of love and loyalty, like soccer stud David Beckham's pictures of his wife, Victoria, three cherubs representing his children, and ten roses for his tenth wedding anniversary. Some serve as remembrances, like rapper Lil Wayne's teardrops, representing deaths of loved ones; or a *Miami Ink* customer's blue heron, a remembrance of the one that flew by her mother's hospital window every day when she was battling cancer.

Some tattoos show solidarity. A soldier's tattoo pays tribute to his squadron, homage to the men who had his back in battle; while a barista we met at a coffee shop has a Robert Frost quote printed on her forearm that salutes another squadron: her family. Some cover up past mistakes. Johnny Depp had "Winona Forever" inked on his arm. Turns out "Forever" lasted about three years; after he and Winona Ryder broke off their engagement, Depp had the tattoo altered to read "Wino Forever."

An estimated 45 million Americans have endured the pain of marking their bodies in order to tell us something of their stories. And although the other 268 million may not have their skin permanently inked, the truth is, we've all been marked by pain.

As therapists living and working in a diverse university town, we hear firsthand the real-life stories reflected in the mental health statistics reported by the American College Health Association about what this marking pain looks like. The ACHA polls more than one hundred thousand students across the country. At some point during the twelve months leading up to the last survey, college students reported:

- 86.3% felt overwhelmed by all they had to do.
- 61.1% felt very sad.
- 57.3% felt very lonely.
- 50.6% felt overwhelming anxiety.
- 45.1% felt that things were hopeless.
- 37.1% felt overwhelming anger.

All of us can relate. We've all been branded by something called humanity, and none of us survive it unmarked by some pain, loss, and disappointment. Whatever the source, the perforations etched into our minds will influence the way we experience the world. We're all going to be marked by something; the good news is that we have the power to choose to be permeated by the imprint of something positive, holy, strong: God's love. All of us can.

In the process of writing this book about how we can choose God's mark to transform our lives, an interesting thing happened. We started seeing tattoos everywhere we went. We became bold in asking our waiters, the salesclerk at the department store, the volunteer at the animal shelter, and strangers at the coffee shop to tell us the stories behind their tattoos. As we did, something amazing unfolded. People started talking to us about their internal tattoos.

We got to know people in a way that we wouldn't have otherwise. We cried with the salesclerk who explained that the cursive "Serenity" inked on the inside of her wrist was connected with her freedom from addiction. We were surprised to find that the tattoo peeking out of the teenager's T-shirt sleeve was a replica of a famous Renaissance painting of the archangel Michael—and surprised again to learn of how he had struggled with poverty and mental illness in his immediate family. We sat in our colorist's chair with foil in our hair, learning that the apple tree branch with apples running the length of her calf symbolized those closest to her. It turns out many people will endure the pain of a needle repeatedly injected into their skin to create a permanent image if that image has deep meaning to them.

We also heard many tattoo stories that reflected a turning point in a life—a time when a person decided, despite past hurt, to be changed. Our friend Hope lived through a childhood marked by poverty, addiction, and abuse. Growing up in a one-room apartment surrounded by drug-addicted relatives, Hope was exposed to pornographic videos and sexually abused from the time she was about seven years old. She often worried about how she'd get her next meal. By the time she was fourteen, she was drinking and smoking. During her teen years, her future seemed bleak—until something miraculous happened. She fell in love. Colin loved Hope unconditionally and came from a Christian family who also loved her unconditionally.

Hope said she first fell in love with the Jesus she saw in Colin. More than anything, she wanted what he had in Jesus. Through the transforming power of Christ, she overcame seemingly insurmountable odds and since has been the director of a nonprofit counseling center and has served months at a time in the slums of Calcutta. Today she is a psychiatric nurse visiting patients in their homes to make sure they are safe and taking their medications. Once poor, addicted, and abandoned herself, she is now serving the poor, addicted, and abandoned.

One night, wanting to commemorate their wedding anniversary, Hope and Colin decided to get tattoos. After getting up the next morning and seeing the cross with vines stamped on her lower back, Hope questioned the wisdom of her decision. She wondered if it was a mistake. But, since it was permanent, she started praying to God that she could somehow use her tattoo as a witness to God's work in her life. Then one day, she came across this passage in Lamentations 3:19-23:

I remember my affliction and my wandering,
  the bitterness and the gall.
I well remember them,
  and my soul is downcast within me.
Yet this I call to mind
  and therefore I have hope:
Because of the LORD's great love we are not consumed,
  for his compassions never fail.
They are new every morning;
  great is your faithfulness. (NIV)

Those words, written by Jeremiah almost twenty-six hundred years ago, after the fall of Jerusalem, remarkably reflect Hope's own personal history—the destruction of her past, and God's great faithfulness in rebuilding her life into something new. She went back to the tattoo artist and asked him to write this above the cross and vines:

Hope's story reminds us that we don't have to let the stains and smudges of our pasts permanently discolor us. While she could have spent her life accepting the marks of guilt, addiction, poverty, and abuse, instead she chose to be pierced by God's love and to be permeated by God's imprint.

We'll each share later about some of the ways we've been marked, but what about you? What kind of ink has colored your life?

Even if our stories aren't as dramatic as Hope's, we've all been up against our own odds. Even those of us who don't have a physical tattoo for all the world to see have still been pierced and stained by pain.

Sharon was marked by the cruel comments of her high school choir director, when he made an offhand joke about how she needed to lay off the pizza. She took his words to heart and nearly starved herself to death in a long battle with anorexia. From the time Ben was a boy, he was marked by his father's criticisms and was told that he'd never amount to anything. He spent most of his adulthood trying to overcome the stabs that chipped away at his self-image. Nichole's parents viewed everything she did through the filter of how her sister did it first or better or smarter. She strives to set herself apart from her sister's accomplishments and establish her own mark on the world.

In spite of events that are *so* deeply etched into our hearts, we have the power to change the marks that life makes on us.

A cold-blooded source of pain threatened to permanently discolor Viktor Frankl's future, and he had a tattoo to memorialize it. It was a simple number on his arm—119104—a number given to him by Nazi soldiers when he was suddenly forced into the horror of a World War II concentration camp. While a prisoner, he was stripped of everything he owned—his possessions, his identity as a prominent psychiatrist, and his pride. He suffered the loss of his wife and friends to the death chambers. He was malnourished to the point of becoming almost a walking skeleton and forced to perform hard labor in extreme conditions. Documenting his survival and lessons he learned in his classic book *Man's Search for Meaning*, he said, "Everything can be taken from a man but one thing: the last of the human freedoms—to choose one's attitude in any given set of circumstances, to choose one's own way."

More than a trite philosophical idea, that statement was made by a man who survived the most inhumane treatment from his fellow human beings.

Now, the idea that we can choose our own way, that we can reink the marks that have been made on our lives, is an ancient concept. During the time of Roman emperor Nero's persecutions, the apostle Paul wrote from prison urging the first-century Christians to be transformed by the renewing of their minds. In the Gospel of John, we see the most dramatic picture of a word becoming flesh. Not just any word—*the* Word. Christ. John wrote, "The Word became flesh and made his home among us." This book is about the power of imprinting that Word on our lives.

People are sometimes surprised when we explain that we use stories and slang from tattoo culture as a way to look at how Christ desires that we be inked by him. But an estimated one quarter of Americans ages eighteen to fifty have a tattoo. What better way to show how one of the most polarizing of cultural icons can, in fact, be a metaphor for what we have in common?

The apostle Paul debated with early converts to the faith about another kind of polarizing outward mark (religious circumcision). He said what really counts is a new creation. He pointed to the scars on his body from the whippings he endured for the right to become a new creation and essentially said, "Don't cause me any grief about this—because I bear on my body the marks of Jesus." In his message *Tattoo*, speaker Louie Giglio also reminds us of our inner choice to be imprinted by God when he says, "God is less interested in what's on your arm than he is in what's going on in your heart. Arms are easy; hearts are tough!"

We all have marks that have been made on our hearts. And at the end of each chapter, we'll give you a chance to reflect with a few questions or suggestions under the heading "Engrave It!" It is our deep hope that we all choose to allow the Word that was made flesh to change those marks so that we can live as new creations—in the permanent words of Hope's tattoo, *against all odds*.

Showcases: Choosing Your Artist

They are . . . the work of my hands,

for the display of my splendor.

—Isaiah 60:21 (NIV)

One of the last tattoos I got is . . . a picture of Jesus's face superimposed over a cross. He's on the same leg with the demon with no eyes. When I look at myself now, I see what I couldn't see then. This was spiritual warfare, taking place subconsciously on my body. The soulless demon. The face of Jesus. The battle had begun.

—Josh Hamilton

Tattoos were first introduced to the United States when German-born Martin Hildebrandt tattooed both Union and Confederate soldiers in their camps. Tattooing reached its "golden age" in the 1940s when sailors returned home sporting their new body art. Tattoo popularity spread to include bikers in the 1950s, hippies in the 1960s, rock stars in the 1970s and 1980s, and athletes in the 1990s. Now, tattoos have become part of the mainstream. According to the Pew Research Center, 40 percent of people born between 1961 and 1981 have at least one tattoo.

For the 60 percent who don't have a tattoo, Josh Hamilton has done his share of picking up the slack. But long before the star outfielder for the Texas Rangers ever thought of getting the first of his twenty-six tattoos, Josh was marked by a dream to play baseball. At six years old, he was throwing a baseball at fifty miles per hour—so fast that the other parents complained that their kids were in danger of being hurt. The Tar Heel League bumped him up to his brother's team of fifth through seventh graders.

As a teen, Josh was ranked by *Baseball America* among the top five high school players in the country. He was so heavily scouted that he even missed his senior prom in order to avoid any potential scandals.

At eighteen years old, just two days after his high school graduation, Josh was drafted—as the number one pick in 1999—by the Tampa Bay Devil Rays. The dream that had marked his early childhood was becoming a reality, and he inked a record $3.96 million signing bonus.

In his book *Beyond Belief: Finding the Strength to Come Back*, Josh explained that his original ink began to be smudged when he was in a major car accident in 2001, resulting in a back injury. Unable to play the sport he loved and being isolated from his family, Josh began frequenting a tattoo shop in a Tampa strip mall; it became his second home. In tattoo lingo, showcases are people who display on their bodies a lot of work from the same artist. Now, with nothing but time and money, Josh would spend hours in the chair, numbing out, letting the artist decide what he wanted to ink onto Hamilton's body. He was fast becoming a showcase for that artist, and the marks would prove to be more than skin-deep.

Josh's story has similarities to the story of the twelve Israelite spies. When God brought the Israelites out of slavery and was ready to bring them to the land he had promised them, Moses was instructed to select a leader from each of the twelve tribes to go and stake out the land. After forty days of exploring the land, its towns, its people, and its vegetation, they came back and

reported this to Moses: "We went into the land to which you sent us, and it does flow with milk and honey! . . . But the people who live there are powerful, and the cities are fortified and very large." Only Caleb said, "We should go up and take possession of the land, for we can certainly do it." But the Bible says that those against Caleb spread fear throughout the Israelites, saying, "The land we explored devours those living in it. All the people we saw there are of great size. . . . We seemed like grasshoppers in our own eyes, and we looked the same to them."

Josh did what so many of us do. We imprint on our minds that we are grasshoppers. Then those around us see that ink and treat us according to the mark we've taken on for ourselves—that we are small, insignificant, a failure. And what does that tell people about the Artist we're showcasing? The Bible says we are "God's handiwork," "the work of [his] hand," and created for the display of his splendor." Do we believe that? What's more, do we really allow it to change the way we identify ourselves? Does it challenge us to live differently, to go forth and take possession of whatever God has promised for our own lives?

Which Artist Is in Charge?

When asked to explain the meaning behind each of his twenty-six tattoos, Josh half laughs. "The truth is, most of the time I wasn't interested in what they were putting on my body . . . *the artists were in charge.*" And, left in charge, what they inked included a number of demons on his body. He said that what started out as a release eventually became another master to obey—a master that first showed up in a premonition during his first summer in the pros.

He was playing center field at a night game and a thunderstorm was looming. He describes it like this:

> There was lightning in the distance, and the clouds lit up every few seconds as they bounced our way. I watched, interested in the formations and curious about whether they would arrive and wash out the game.
>
> I have difficulty describing what happened next. The clouds kept moving, and suddenly a demon's face appeared, superimposed on the clouds. It was jumping out at me, and it made me rock back on my heels. I got chills. The face was grinning, almost taunting.
>
> The vision stuck with me the rest of the game. I didn't know what to make of it, but I didn't feel I could ignore it. There was something there for me, some message or warning.

After the game, walking back to the motel, he and his roommate noticed a bluish light coming from their room. They both remembered turning off the TV and all the lights. Nothing seemed amiss when they entered their room. His roommate headed straight for the bathroom and Josh went to turn on the TV. What he saw stopped him dead in his tracks. There on the hotel television,

Hamilton reports that he saw an image of clouds similar to what he had witnessed from the ball field. Except this time, rather than a demon, he believed he was seeing Jesus, reaching out to him.

Feeling that this was obviously connected with what had happened during the game, Josh felt that he was being sent a message and that it was his job to figure out what it was. "So, with the events of that night providing the push, I lay in bed in a West Virginia motel room and thought seriously about the role of Jesus Christ in my life, and how I was supposed to respond to His message."

It seemed as if he might then begin to choose some different marks for his life, but somewhere between the deep impressions of that night and October 2005, Josh decided to showcase a different artist.

The next few years were gouged by drug abuse, baseball suspensions, rehab stays, hospital visits, dangerous threats from drug dealers, and the heartbreak of those who loved him.

On a fateful day in October 2005, Josh woke up after a crack binge in a hot trailer surrounded by strangers. He had loaned his truck to a dealer to get more crack, but the dealer hadn't come back. He walked trancelike down a two-lane highway and eventually found a pay phone, where he called his estranged wife, Katie, for a ride. Josh said, "I was a bad husband and a bad father, and I had no relationship with God. Baseball wasn't even on my mind." But on the ride home, Katie told him about a dream she had—one where God impressed upon her that He was going to bring Josh back to baseball, but that it wouldn't be about baseball. It would be for something much bigger. Josh blew her off.

While Katie believed that God was going to bring Josh back to baseball for something bigger, she wasn't ready to let him come home. With nowhere else to go, Josh showed up at his granny's house. Mary Holt, who had always provided a safe haven when he was a little boy, took one look at Josh's wrecked body and said, "I'm tired of you killing yourself. I'm tired of watching you hurt all of these people who care about you." She took him in and forced him to rest, and for the next few months, she nourished him back to physical and emotional health. God used her as an instrument in the process of reinking the original etches that had marked the early years of Josh's life.

It wouldn't be easy, though; the smudges and smears of the ink he'd been showcasing were stubbornly stamped on his being. That first week, Josh had a nightmare, which he related to an interviewer:

> I was fighting the devil, an awful-looking thing. I had a stick or a bat or something, and every time I hit the devil, he'd fall and get back up. Over and over I hit him, until I was exhausted and he was still standing. I woke up in a sweat, as if I'd been truly fighting, and the terror that gripped me makes that dream feel real to this day. I'd been alone for so long, alone with the fears and emotions I worked so hard to kill. I'm not embarrassed to admit that after I woke up that night, I walked down the hall to my grandmother's room and crawled under the covers with her.

The next night, Josh picked up a Bible at the foot of his bed and asked God for help. He came across this verse: "Submit

yourselves, then, to God. Resist the devil, and he will flee from you." "The devil stayed out of my dreams for seven months after that," Josh said. "I stayed clean and worked hard and tried to put my marriage and my life back together."

Grasshoppers or Conquerors?

Josh desperately wanted to get back to playing baseball, but his more recent past was chiseled into his memory, and he was afraid of again disappointing those who loved him. One day while eating at the kitchen table while his granny did the dishes, he told her he didn't think he'd ever play baseball again. As he tells it, his granny turned back to the dishes and smiled to herself. She would tell him later that it was at that point that she knew he was at least *thinking* about ball, and that she knew that meant he'd get back to *playing* ball.

Crediting God and Granny's approach to rehab, Josh was sober for eight months and returned to baseball in June 2006. A few weeks later, the devil reappeared in the same old dream, but with an important difference. Josh said,

> I would hit him and he would bounce back up, the ugliest and most hideous creature you could imagine. This devil seemed unbeatable; I couldn't knock him out. But just when I felt like giving up, I felt a presence by my side. I turned my head and saw Jesus, battling alongside me. We kept fighting, and I was filled with strength. The devil didn't stand a chance. You can doubt me, but I swear to you I dreamed it. When I woke up, I felt

at peace. I wasn't scared. To me, the lesson was obvious. Alone, I couldn't win this battle. With Jesus, I couldn't lose.

About 275 years after the Israelites had crossed the Jordan to claim God's promise for them, they would again face what looked like giants. For seven years, they had been hiding in caves from the Midianites, who would invade and destroy their livestock and crops. The Bible says the Israelites finally cried out to the Lord for help and, once again, God came to their rescue. The angel of the Lord found Gideon—hiding in a winepress, threshing wheat there so the Midianites wouldn't discover it. And when the angel of the Lord found Gideon, this is what he said to him: "The LORD is with you, mighty warrior."

Mighty warrior? That's not a tattoo Gideon remembered getting. He was hiding out in a winepress, for crying out loud! Even Gideon thought it was ludicrous (one might even say as ludicrous as calling a crack addict a Major League Baseball All-Star). He said, "What do you mean, God's sending me to save Israel from the Midianites? I'm from the weakest clan and, not only that, I'm the least in my family!"

Then again, this is the same God who "calls things that don't exist into existence." The rest of Gideon's story and the miraculous battle against the Midianites is in Judges 6 and 7, but the bottom line is that God did, indeed, use Gideon to lead just three hundred men to defeat what many scholars estimate must have been hundreds of thousands of enemy soldiers. This time, instead of doubting grasshoppers turning away from God's plan, mighty conquerors were born of faithfulness to God's calling.

"Addiction is a humbling experience," Josh admitted.

> Getting it under control is even more humbling. I got better for one reason: I surrendered. Instead of asking to be bailed out, instead of making deals with God by saying, "If you get me out of this mess, I'll stop doing what I'm doing," I asked for help. I wouldn't do that before. I'd been the Devil Rays' No. 1 pick in the 1999 draft, supposedly a five-tool prospect. I was a big, strong man, and I was supposed to be able to handle my problems myself. That didn't work out so well.

No matter what happened in the future, Josh had finally rejected his grasshopper tendencies and had become God's warrior, claiming God's true mark for his life.

Eight months later, he was once again playing in the majors, ultimately for the Texas Rangers. On July 14, 2008, which he has described as one of the most exhilarating nights of his life, he hit twenty-eight homers in the Home Run Derby in Yankee Stadium (the next highest was eight) while the crowd chanted, "Ham-il-ton. Ham-il-ton. Ham-il-ton." Two weeks prior, playing the Yankees in New York, the crowd had chanted, "Josh smokes crack. Josh smokes crack." But, like Gideon, Josh Hamilton isn't after the applause of men; he's chosen to showcase the Master Artist.

There was yet another Israelite who learned the importance of showcasing the right artist over listening to man's opinion. He had three older brothers in the army, fighting in a battle twenty miles or so southwest of Jerusalem. One day, in the hopes of getting some firsthand news from the front line, he delivered food to his brothers and their commanding officer. When he arrived in the valley where the battle was taking place, he learned that the enemy had made an unusual challenge: "Our best soldier against yours in a single combat. The winner of the match determines the outcome. If our soldier kills your challenger, you accede to our demands; if your soldier is victorious, we'll surrender."

It was a tempting wager. As uncommon as it was, if a soldier could prevail in the challenge, many resources and lives would be spared. There was only one problem: no soldier was willing to volunteer for the task.

Then this young man showed up. He was incredulous: "Who does this guy think he is, insulting Israel's army?" When he offered to take up the challenge in this one-to-one combat, he was mocked by his own brothers and dismissed as naive by the commander in chief of Israel's armed forces. Refusing to allow that ink to penetrate his thinking, the boy swore that before the day was over, he'd have the challenger's head. And he picked up his weapon and did just that.

The year was around 1024 B.C. The place was the Elah Valley. The boy's name was David, and his weapon was a slingshot. Before David killed Goliath, he made it perfectly clear whom he was showcasing: "This day the whole world will know there is a God in Israel!"

As Josh Hamilton told us in a phone interview, when the fans voted him into the 2008 All-Star game, he didn't feel as though he deserved it compared to other players. He said he prayed about it and that it was impressed upon him that he would be given the opportunity to showcase Christ. At the end of the Home Run Derby, Erin Andrews, reporting for ESPN, did, indeed, approach him and asked him what had been the most memorable event of this season, the All-Star game, and the Home Run Derby. Josh said, "I just got this big grin on my face and said that it has been sharing Christ with millions of people."

Josh has many trophies in his showcase—four-time All-Star, American League MVP, American League Players Choice Award for Outstanding Player, *USA Today* American League Most Valuable Player, the Silver Slugger Award, the American League batting champion, *and* the American League Champion Series MVP. Yet, like David slaying the giant so that the whole world would know there is a God in Israel, Josh is interested only in showcasing his Artist. Of God, Josh said: "He's not worried about accolades, or trophies, or anything like that. He's worried about how can I glorify Him in everything I do." Josh also said,

> This may sound crazy, but I wouldn't change a thing about my path to the big leagues. I wouldn't even change the 26 tattoos that cover so much of my body, even though they're the most

> obvious signs of my life temporarily leaving the tracks. You're probably thinking, "Bad decisions and addiction almost cost him his life, and he wouldn't change anything?" But if I hadn't gone through all the hard times, this whole story would be just about baseball. If I'd made the big leagues at 21 and made my first All-Star team at 23 and done all the things expected of me, I would be a big-time baseball player, and that's it. Baseball is third in my life right now, behind my relationship with God and my family. Without the first two, baseball isn't even in the picture. Believe me, I know.

At the outset, a showcase for himself. For a time, a showcase for the enemy. Now, a walking showcase for God. He said, "If I had stayed that clean-cut kid, people would listen to me, but *how many more people* am I able to reach because I've lived those things? I don't encourage people to get tattoos, and I wouldn't get another one, but I wouldn't be here if they weren't here. They're my battle scars." Josh Hamilton now uses those battle scars to glorify God every chance he gets: to churches and youth organizations, to readers of *GQ* magazine and *Sports Illustrated,* to viewers of CNN and ESPN, and to millions of fans who cheer him on as he walks up to the plate.

As he told us, "There's a bigger picture . . . and it's not baseball."

The ink we allow to permeate our thinking affects who we become. With the help of his granny, Josh allowed the mark of God to fill up the ruts that had been engraved by the enemy, and he was able to reclaim the very thing he had been made for.

The freed Israelites marked themselves as grasshoppers, ignoring God's call for their lives. As a result, what would have been an eleven-day trip from slavery to the Promised Land turned into forty years of wandering and grumbling in the desert. In contrast, Gideon eventually allowed God's imprint of a mighty warrior to seep into his thinking and he ended up leading the Israelites to freedom once again—against the odds.

We choose what marks are engraved on our minds. But so many of us passively allow the ruts to be grooved until we are like elephants in captivity. A baby elephant in captivity is often tied to a tree with a heavy rope or chain. At first, he tries with all his might to break free—but to no avail. He keeps falling down until he finally gives up—for the rest of his life. Later, when he's an adult, all his captors need do is tie him to a tree. The tree doesn't even have to be big, and the rope doesn't have to be strong. Even though the elephant has the physical strength to uproot the tree and free himself, the marks of his past experiences have been too deeply gouged into his memory for him to believe he has any alternative.

We often see ourselves as grasshoppers and not as mighty warriors. Do we believe in a God who uses the unlikeliest to fulfill his mission? Do we believe that a God who used a small band of men to defeat hundreds of thousands and who brought a baseball player back from a crack addiction to the World Series can fill up the marks of our lives and turn us into showcases of God's splendor? We allow our past experiences to create such deep grooves into our thinking, but God might yet mark our lives differently.

I will become whatever image I hold of myself and life, and therefore I will picture what I can be when filled with the Lord's power.

—Lloyd John Ogilvie, former chaplain to the US Senate

Engrave It!

Grab a journal or a pad of paper and carve out some time for personal reflection. List the following:

1. *Abilities.* Try not to filter or judge yourself, but simply list all of your abilities—academic, artistic, athletic, social, and other skills. This is no time to be humble; list as many abilities as you can!
2. *Accomplishments.* Have you put yourself through college, started a small business, overcome a fear, learned a second language? Recognize every accomplishment you can remember as well as the energy that you put into those endeavors.
3. *Experiences.* List the experiences that have made a major impact on your life—positive or negative.
4. *God's Word.* Grab a Bible and brainstorm a list of verses that describe who God says you are from God's word. For a good starting point, check out Ephesians 2:10; 1 Peter 2:9; and Psalm 139:13-14.
5. *Gifts.* The Bible also says we've all been given unique spiritual gifts. Spend some time reading 1 Corinthians 12 and

Romans 12:6-8. Do any of these verses describe what you think your gift(s) might be? Write them down.

When you're finished, take a break and look at what you've written. What kind of person is emerging? How do you feel about what you see? Journal some thoughts about what God might be trying to showcase about Himself through you.

Flash vs. Custom: Choosing the Tattoo Worthy

Do not conform any longer to the pattern of this world,

but be transformed by the renewing of your mind.

—Romans 12:2 (NIV)

Think Before You Ink!
(sign often seen in tattoo shops)

Ricky is nineteen years old—handsome, with blue eyes, fair skin, and soft blond curls peeping out of his knitted cap. Tall and slender, he towers over his pretty girlfriend, laughing and swinging her hand. A tattoo peeks out of the top of Ricky's V-neck T-shirt—the treble clef–like symbol for *Hakuna Matata*.

Hakuna Matata is the Swahili phrase made popular by *The Lion King* that, loosely translated, means "no worries." Based on his tattoo, we might guess that Ricky's life has been marked by carefree ease and security. But we would be wrong.

Ricky knows what it is to have everything taken but the ability to choose one's own way. His developmental years were marked by chaos, neglect, and addiction. In one of his earliest memories (around six, he guesses), he is wailing and beating on a picture window to get his mother's attention. She never turns around, but pulls out of the driveway, leaving Ricky and his younger siblings alone with a man she barely knows so she can go barhopping.

What kind of mark is cut into a little boy's heart when his mother leaves him with a strange man for her own selfish pursuits? Probably some of the negative messages we all struggle with: that the world is unsafe, that we are unlovable, that our needs aren't important. For Ricky, it was at that moment he was imprinted with the belief that he could not depend on his mother.

When Ricky was seventeen, his mother announced that she and his siblings were moving to another city. He could have moved with her, except the most extraordinary of things had happened. Despite the pain that had marked his childhood, he had decided to choose for himself the ink that would mark the rest of his life.

Ricky had surprised teachers and school counselors alike by working hard to raise his failing grades to a 3.4 GPA. He had become the poster child for high school dropout prevention, he had a job that he took very seriously, and he planned to go to college. He was in a good place; he couldn't just leave it. After his mother left, Ricky slept on his father's couch for a week, but since his father was under house arrest for drug charges, the court wouldn't allow him to live there. So Ricky left with everything he owned in a black garbage bag, suddenly homeless.

Yet again, he had to decide if he was going to be marked by defeat or choose his own ink. Ricky said, "After my safety net was removed, I had to decide: was I going to fall or fly?" He chose to fly. He found a two-year program that provides housing to homeless youth and helps them transition to successful independent living. He is substance-free, he's halfway through college, is a model employee, and is now living successfully on his own.

Ricky said that the moment he realized he had nowhere to go, no one who cared whether or not he succeeded, no one who would be telling him what to do, he knew it was up to him to choose his own way. He said his next tattoo will be a quote from the movie *Fight Club*: "It's only after we've lost everything that we are free to do anything."

> *Jack Sparrow: One question about your business, boy, or there's no use going: This girl . . . how far are you willing to go to save her?*
>
> *Will Turner: I'd die for her.*
>
> *Jack Sparrow: Oh good. No worries then.*
>
> —Pirates of the Caribbean: The Curse of the Black Pearl

We can go through life one of two ways. We can choose the kind of ink that marks pirate Jack Sparrow, who sees the upshot of everything, or we can go through life choosing the ink of Davy Jones, who rips out his heart, places it in a chest, and buries it after suffering extreme disappointment. We too can be mad at the world for our circumstances and lock our hearts up in a chest that's buried in the depths of the earth. Savvy?

And it has nothing to do with our circumstances. Jack Sparrow's life is marked by women troubles, a drinking problem, career displacement, legal issues, and at one point a deranged mind. Yet he always seems to spin his circumstances to the positive ("This is the day that you will always remember as the day that you *almost* caught Captain Jack Sparrow!"). And when we find him *At World's End* surrounded by dozens of Jack Sparrow copies, figments of his imagination, what tattoo is revealed on the bare back of one of his clones? "Desiderata"—a poem full of wisdom about living optimistically. A poem that, among its last lines, includes: "With all its sham, drudgery, and broken dreams, it is still a beautiful world."

But life is no Disney movie, and it can leave us stained by some pretty messed-up ink. There are plenty of people who love God heart and soul, but who still struggle with food issues, addictions, and abusive relationships. Some people carry so much emotional pain it seems their only release is through self-injury. Others are twisted with anxiety about their future. So, how do we think we can change our lives by simply taking charge of the ink that permeates our thinking?

Well, for starters, we're not the only ones to believe it true. William James, a nineteenth-century psychologist, is attributed as saying that the greatest discovery of his generation was that human beings could alter their lives by altering their attitudes of mind. Change your attitude; change your life.

The greatest discovery of his generation? Could be an easy claim to gloss over, unless we think about the other great discoveries of his generation. They include penicillin, the introduction of antiseptic in surgery to avoid infection, the first use of anesthetics on humans, the rabies vaccination, the discovery of the double-helix structure of DNA, pasteurization, the first EKG machine, $E = MC^2$, the periodic table of elements, X-rays, the Ferris wheel, the elevator, motion pictures, the telephone, chewing gum, and the first toilet paper on a roll! (And the list goes on.) Pretty amazing

discoveries, but it's said that James thought the *greatest* discovery was the realization that we can change our lives by changing our attitudes!

Yet there was one who discovered this truth long before the 1800s, despite a life marked by incredible obstacles. Like Jack Sparrow, this man's obstacles included shipwreck, but any comparison to a story inked by Hollywood ends there. His real-life story was marked by wrongful imprisonment, severe beatings, homelessness, hard labor, hunger, poverty, and betrayal. Serious coverage by some ugly ink.

Yet he wrote *this* in one of his letters from prison:

> I want you to know that the things that have happened to me have actually advanced the gospel. . . . I have learned how to be content in any circumstance. I know the experience of being in need and of having more than enough; I have learned the secret to being content in any and every circumstance, whether full or hungry or whether having plenty or being poor.

Instead of being defeated by the marks on his life, the apostle Paul chose to "think about the things above and not things on earth." Although he had suffered the gashes of some bad ink, what mattered to him was God's design for his life. The gospel was being advanced and souls were being saved, "*whatever* the circumstances." Reminds us of some others who were able to say *whatever*:

- *Abraham Lincoln:* Marked by business failure, political defeat (for the legislature as well as for the vice presidency), the death of his sweetheart, and a nervous breakdown, yet he persisted and became our sixteenth president in 1860. He said, "I want it said of me by those who knew me best, that I always plucked a thistle and planted a flower where I thought a flower would grow."

- *Viktor Frankl:* He and his fellow concentration camp prisoners were marked by physical and emotional suffering, the plundering of their material possessions, the executions of their families, and the loss of freedom, yet he wrote that men would still walk through the huts giving comfort and even their last piece of bread to others. He said, "They may have been few in number, but they offer sufficient proof that everything can be taken away from a man but one thing: the last of human freedoms—to choose one's attitude in any set of circumstances, to choose one's own way."
- *Helen Keller:* Marked by deafness and blindness from nineteen months old, she chose not to let her disability defeat her, but became the first blind and deaf person to earn a bachelor of arts degree. She became a writer, speaker, political activist, and advocate for people with disabilities. She said, "Only through experiences of trial and suffering can the soul be strengthened, vision cleared, ambition inspired, and success achieved."
- *Walt Disney:* He created Mickey Mouse at a time when business fortunes were at their lowest ebb and disaster seemed right around the corner. He also said that he never

tried anything new unless at least a hundred people told him it couldn't be done, and that all the adversity he'd ever had in life had really served to strengthen him: "You may not realize it when it happens, but a kick in the teeth may be the best thing in the world for you."

- Joseph the Patriarch: His life was marked by betrayal by his own brothers, slavery in a foreign land, false accusations of rape, and wrongful imprisonment in a dungeon. Yet when he was reunited with his brothers he was able to say, "You planned something bad for me, but God produced something good from it, in order to save the lives of many people."

Take a look at those around you. No doubt we can all name at least one person who's been marked by disadvantage, yet who always seems to have a positive outlook and is overcoming his circumstances against the craziest kinds of odds. On the other hand, we can also name someone who has been marked by an affluence of material and social resources. Afforded every opportunity, he still seems miserable and often makes those around him miserable.

So, what's the difference? How do some of us take our stains, smears, and smudges and turn them into the hallmark of a success story, whereas others allow that same ink to infect their minds and hearts so that they are oozing toxins everywhere they walk? Paul said, "I have learned the secret of being content in any and every situation." Can't you just hear Paul whispering, "Psst, over here . . . I have a secret to tell you—something monumental that will change your life"? So we hold our breath while he completes his thought: "I can endure all these things through the power of the one who gives me strength." Whatever the circumstances.

We all have a whatever. Some bad ink has been scratched in and it's now turned into an infected blotch. But we can clean it up, let it heal, and then turn it into a testament of triumph. It is possible to choose. Say, *"Whatever. . . . Bring it on. I can handle anything, because it's Jesus who gives me strength."*

Flash vs. Custom

Walk into any tattoo shop and, if you haven't given much thought to your design, you can look through any number of catalogs or the art hanging on the walls behind cheap plastic frames and select from their flash. Flash is stock art, unoriginal. Flash is easy. The world is full of flash. Flash is what gets inked onto our brains when we're not paying attention. It's the messages we take in day after day without even questioning their truth or usefulness or what they're doing to our spirits. Flash is what others choose for us.

When our friend Ellen was getting her first tattoo, the artist told her that most females come to him to get a single word tattooed on their wrist, something like *Faith* or *Love*, sometimes in another language to put a twist on it. He said that if he had to do another one, he thought he might just go crazy. Another artist told us that he really likes it when someone brings him a design that surprises him, especially one that is playful or makes him

laugh. Most tattoo artists like creativity and originality; they don't like doing flash.

Neither does God. He's not a one-size-fits-all hack who bought some starter tattoo kit off the internet. He's an Artist who numbers the hairs on our heads, who records our every tear, who perceives our thoughts from afar, knows the very next words we're going to speak before they even leave our mouths, and who set us apart before we were born. We're not talking about a guy who pulls out a three-ring binder from under the counter or points to the wall and lets you select another run-of-the-mill STOMA (Something Tribal on My Arm). This is the Artist who says we are a masterpiece.

And this Artist who says we are a masterpiece, who makes only custom work, wants us to choose custom work. Custom work is what the apostle Paul is talking about when he says, "Do not conform any longer to the pattern of this world, but be transformed by the renewing of your mind." We're bombarded daily with flash, but it is possible to choose custom work.

One night, during a particularly difficult time in her life, Kim couldn't sleep. An important relationship was being torn apart. We've all been there. Whether it's a friend, a sibling, or a boyfriend or girlfriend, relationship troubles can keep us tossing and turning like someone with the raw flesh of a new tattoo. Kim kept replaying conversations in her mind, wondering where things went wrong, and what could be done to make them right. Minutes, and then hours, ticked away. She begged God to give her sleep, to give her *peace*. Then she remembered this from the apostle Paul's letters to the Philippians: "Whatever is true, whatever is noble, whatever is right, whatever is pure, whatever is lovely, whatever is admirable—if anything is excellent or praiseworthy—think about such things [the *Common English Bible* says "focus your thoughts on these things"]. And the God of peace will be with you." Deciding to put this promise to the test, she considered what she could think of that was pure and lovely. Suddenly, she remembered an image from a few weeks earlier. Focusing with all the concentration of a tattoo artist pressing ink machine to flesh, she recalled the image of her two year old nephew. A couple of weeks before, he had spent the night and the two of them had sat outside on the steps in the summer night air, looking up at the stars and eating donuts.

Kim filled in the outline with every detail she could remember from the scene. She replayed the adorable things her nephew had said. She remembered how he had looked like a miniature sumo wrestler, wearing nothing but a diaper, hunched over with his arms resting on his knees. She remembered how bright the stars were against the black sky. She remembered how the summer air had kissed her skin and had gently blown her hair. She remembered how good it was to bite into that chocolate-covered donut and how the cream filling oozed out. She remembered the utter joy of being in that moment. Just about as pure and lovely as it gets.

And the next thing she knew, it was morning and she was waking up. She had deliberately focused her thoughts on whatever was pure and lovely, and the God of peace had granted her sleep.

More Custom Work

Up until their sons were teenagers, Janet and her husband had been able to raise them in an idyllic small Midwestern town. Time was marked by hanging out with their friends, playing on sports teams, participating in youth group activities, and discovering first loves.

Then the lines got blurred. It started when Janet's husband lost his job because of a failing economy. Weeks went by without him finding another job, and Janet and her husband were becoming visibly more stressed. Eventually, they had to sell the house and tell their sons they had to move to a new town and a new school. Just like that, their lives went from being marked by security to uncertainty.

Janet's husband was actively working toward a solution, but Janet was shocked and confused about the future and having a hard time keeping the ink within the lines—until the seemingly smallest event caused her to get back in focus. She noticed that her plants were nearly dead because she had been neglecting to water them. Realizing that the recent perforations in her life had caused her to become numb, she knew she needed to do something. So she made the slightest move to take charge of the ink machine: she watered her plants. That, in turn, got her to dusting the bookshelves, which was where she noticed a book her grandmother had given her but that she had never read: *The Power of Positive Thinking*.

Reading it in its entirety in one afternoon, Janet learned that she had the power to choose what she would make of the marks on her life. Questions like *why?* only smeared the marks into an indistinguishable pattern; it was time to start focusing on the *whatevers*—in this case, whatever was excellent and praiseworthy.

It was about that time Janet read that the Chinese word for *crisis* has two characters, and they represent two different words: *danger* and *opportunity*. Realizing that her crisis could embody both, Janet began to think of their situation differently. Her family could see that she was becoming more positive and more hopeful about the future, and soon her attitude was contagious.

No longer tied to a geographical area, they had moved to a town where her husband found a job and started a small business. In time, Janet was able to go back to college and pursue her dream of becoming a licensed clinical social worker. Watching their mom grow from the crisis, Janet's children learned that we can choose our attitudes in any given circumstance. We don't have to go with the flash. We can choose custom.

We know it does no good to avoid or deny our problems. Even Jesus said we would have trouble in this world. But we can choose how to react to it. When we are bombarded daily with flash, we can still fill our minds with God's ink. It is possible to choose custom work that is true, noble, right, pure, admirable, excellent, and praiseworthy. Work that is tattoo worthy.

Tattoo Worthy

Once our minds are "tattooed" with negative thinking, our chances for long-term success diminish.

—John Maxwell

When something can stand the test of time and is important enough to justify permanently inking it onto your skin, it's called "Tattoo Worthy." Likewise, there are designs we can ink onto our minds that are "tattoo worthy" . . . and things that are not.

Barbara Fredrickson is director of the Fredrickson Social Psychophysiology Laboratory at the University of Michigan, and she's an expert about what is "tattoo worthy." Tapping into one of our most common fears, she forced nervousness in the participants of one study by telling them that they were going to have to give a speech. She then measured their cardiovascular reactions. She repeated the measurements after showing some of them video images such as playful puppies and waves lapping on the beach. She observed that participants returned to normal cardiovascular levels after seeing the video.

We would expect that. But what she also learned was that you don't get the same result just by taking participants' minds off the negative, fear-producing thought. *The thought must be replaced by something positive.* Knowing that our thinking affects all aspects of our lives, including our faith, our health, our self-esteem, our educations, our careers, and our relationships, how do we make tattoo-worthy choices?

Unplug

Kim was at a concert when the up-and-coming young artist announced that he was going to sing, for the first time, a song to his girlfriend for their first anniversary. As the fans oohed and ahhed, he quieted them with these words:

> Could we, just once, turn off the cell phones and not video this? Could it not show up on YouTube? We spend so much time videoing life, we're not experiencing it. And, I don't know, it seems like things are less pure when we can watch them over and over again on video. And, could this just be between us? Because I think there's something really cool about knowing that no one else will experience this moment—just us, in this room. And it's like, I don't know, have you ever had a cool discussion with your parents, or an experience where if you had videoed it, it wouldn't be the same as it is in your memory? Some things are just more special when we can only have them in our memories. And, oh yeah, could I have total silence?

Cell phones disappeared into bags and back pockets as everyone hushed and cleared a path so that his girlfriend, standing at the back of the crowd, could hear her anniversary song. It was a beautiful thing.

Researchers at the University of South Carolina are using brain scans to discover how our emotional responses are altered when we receive hundreds of messages a day via text, e-mail, Twitter, and Facebook. One doctor from Johns Hopkins reported that "we were not made to interact like that" and said that all this social media activity is linked to the high number of anxiety disorders and anxiety prescriptions. At the least, he advises compartmentalizing the time we spend sending and receiving electronic messages. If we have to check Facebook to see if our friend is going through a breakup, maybe it's time we took a break from technology and went outside to play.

Play

Albert Einstein said that play is the highest form of research. And he wasn't talking about the Wii or the Xbox. Play is where discovery happens. The Lascaux Cave paintings and the Dead Sea Scrolls were both discovered by boys playing in caves. What other discoveries lie dormant, waiting for someone with a playful spirit to discover them?

Like salve on a raw tattoo, outdoor play has been described as a "healing balm for the emotional hardships." For example, since the 1800s, the Quakers' Friends Hospital in Pennsylvania has used acres of unspoiled land and a greenhouse to help treat mental illness. There is mounting research that exploring nature has proved therapeutic for attention-deficit disorders, anxiety, and other ills. Richard Louv wrote in *Last Child in the Woods* that more than one hundred studies confirm the relationship between time spent in nature and stress reduction.

Today, therapists and pharmaceutical companies charge hundreds of dollars to treat our anxiety. But the book of Job gave a pro bono prescription an estimated four thousand years ago: "Stop and consider God's wonders."

Laugh

Proving the proverb that a joyful heart helps healing, scientists now know that laughing releases chemicals that boost immunity and reduce the body's level of stress hormones. According to Dr. Caroline Leaf, a good laugh can drop cortisol by 39 percent, reduce adrenaline by 80 percent (too much of either is a bad thing), and increase the "feel-good hormone" endorphin by 29 percent.

Using humor as a "weapon in the fight for self-preservation" in the concentration camp, Viktor Frankl encouraged a man who was working next to him on the building site to make up a funny story every day about what postliberation life might look like. He wrote, "It is well-known that humor, more than anything else in the human make-up, can afford an aloofness and an ability to rise above any situation, even if only for a few seconds."

When's the last time you laughed so hard you cried? A time when onlookers turned out of curiosity (or maybe even envy), wondering what was so funny? Being intentional about inking some humor onto our hearts is tattoo worthy.

More Tattoo Worthy

In addition to unplugging, finding time to play, and discovering reasons to laugh, a lot of research has been done on the positive effects of creative therapies like music therapy, bibliotherapy,

and art therapy. Legendary guitarist Carlos Santana said, "Some songs are just like tattoos for your brain—you hear them and they're affixed to you." And in fact, Viktor Frankl would sing and recite poetry in order to survive the horrors of the concentration camp. But long before these men acknowledged that our thoughts affect our moods, the apostle Paul was the one who wrote that we can be made new in the attitude of our minds.

Our thoughts are imprinted from our experiences, what others say to us, the lyrics we listen to, the movies we watch, and the books we read. Every day, we have the opportunity to choose good markings. To be made new. To choose the tattoo worthy.

Engrave It!

1. How do you need to change how you think about your current situation? Focus on the tattoo worthy. Make a list of at least twenty things that are true, noble, right, pure, lovely, admirable, excellent, or praiseworthy. Whenever you start to have a negative thought, purposefully replace it with something from your list.
2. Doubting the impact of flash ink on our thought lives? Try this experiment. Use an uncommon word or phrase with your friends a few times. Slip it into conversation and pay attention over the next few days to see how many times you start hearing it. Could your positive, encouraging words be just as contagious?

3. The apostle Paul said that the botched marks on his life had really served to advance the gospel. What positive outcomes have or could come from your experience? How can you use your marks as a message to others?

Go outside and play. Do it! Grab a blanket and go outside under the stars tonight, go to an observatory, or take a walk in the woods and turn over some rocks. Wherever. "Stop and consider God's wonders."

Scratcher Tactics: Beware the Hacker

For our struggle is not against flesh and blood, but against the rulers, against the authorities, against the powers of this dark world and against the spiritual forces of evil in the heavenly realms.

—Ephesians 6:12 (NIV)

Good work ain't cheap; cheap work ain't good.

—Norman "Sailor Jerry" Collins, famous tattoo artist

The moment you meet Pete, you get the sense that he's a guy whose life has been marked by some seriously botched-up artwork. He's intimidating. A big guy with a scruffy beard, a scratchy voice, and huge primitive tattoos. Not exactly best-in-show at the tattoo convention. When we met up with him, his driveway was full of cars and motorcycles—biker buddies who had come to hear Pete tell us his story. But Pete and his friends immediately put us at ease as they brought out some folding lawn chairs and sat us where we'd be inside the open garage, shaded from the hot sun.

Pete told us he'd grown up with an abusive, alcoholic father in a low-income neighborhood and was breaking the law by the time he was twelve years old. In the sixties, he joined the biker gang Satan's Preachers, but he won't go into detail about what they did for "entertainment." Because it fit Pete's personality and he liked to drink the cheap alcohol of the same name, a fellow gang member picked a tattoo on Pete's arm by sticking a needle in the eraser end of a pencil, wrapping thread around it, dipping it in ink, and stabbing his skin repeatedly to spell out the words MAD DOG. For about forty years, that was Pete's identity.

On the other hand, Lilly—with her soft blond pixie cut, ivory complexion, and a whopping five foot one in her Chuck Taylors—grew up in middle-class suburbia. A gifted and talented student,

Lilly traveled to Paris with her mother's high school French classes, spent vacations kayaking in the mangroves along the Florida coast with her parents, and taught elementary school girls at a summer camp. She loves British literature, gourmet teas, and her job at a children's hospital. And did we mention she's deeply humble and hilariously funny? At her wedding, after being pronounced husband and wife, she and her husband walked out of the sanctuary to the *Star Wars* theme; then, while guests waited to throw birdseed when they left for their honeymoon, Lilly and her husband surprised them by shooting *them* with water pistols as they ran to the getaway car.

But Lilly has scars too. From a time when she got caught up in a long cycle of cutting in order to numb her feelings. Most of her marks are small and faded, hidden from her family and friends. There's one, though, that would make anyone cringe. At one time, before Lilly met and married the love of her life, she was involved in an emotionally abusive and sexually destructive relationship. One night when she could no longer stand the shame and pain, she carved this inscription into her upper thigh: WHORE.

Pete and Lilly—a middle-aged biker with a criminal record and a twenty-something conservative woman who aspires to be a scholar of Middle English literature—have something in common. They were victims of the Scratcher, what those in the tattoo business sometimes call a hacker, or "an unskilled artist who causes more pain and swelling than necessary."

We've all been victims of the Scratcher, even if we don't have physical tattoos to prove it. Jesus called the Scratcher the father of lies. He deals only with flash, and his tactics haven't changed since the beginning of time.

There are three types of lies the Scratcher will try to gouge into our minds: lies about our true Artist, lies about ourselves, and lies about the world around us. The very first time he shows up, he's slinging all three colors of this poison ink.

The creation account in Genesis is perhaps the best-known Sunday school lesson; an ancient story that's known all over the world, regardless of religious belief. But doesn't it seem strange that God would put two trees in the middle of a garden and tell the first humans, "Here's a good tree and a bad tree. You can have anything you want of everything I've created for you. Just don't eat from that one tree or, oh by the way, you'll die"?

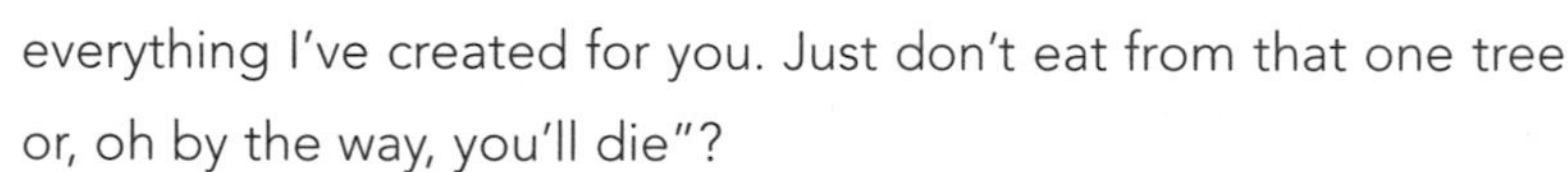

God wants the best for us. Including the free will to love God. Which means we can choose between two things: one a blessing, the other a curse. One, life and prosperity;

the other, death and destruction. And that's a big choice. The biggest.

So when the Scratcher approached Eve with poison ink, intent on hacking a flash design, he stuck to his three best lies, about her true Artist, about herself, and about the world around her. A simple, "Did God *really* say, 'You must not eat from any tree in the garden'?"

Eve tried to resist. But the Scratcher told her more lies. "You won't die! God knows that on the day you eat from it, you will see clearly and you will be like God." With that, Eve succumbed. Adam followed suit, and all humankind after them would suffer the sting of sin and death. But after sin entered the world, God became human in order to save us. Through Jesus, God became our antitoxin: "For the wages of sin is death, but the gift of God is eternal life in Christ Jesus our Lord." And the Scratcher? Not one to give up so quickly, and still bent on our destruction, he moved on to try to thwart God's plan.

In tattoo culture, job stoppers are tattoos that are visible when wearing work attire (such as below the wrist or any area below a skirt's hemline). They may make it difficult to get a job. At the moment Jesus was baptized, the Gospel writers record that heaven opened up, Jesus saw the Spirit of God come down upon him in the form of a dove, and a voice from heaven said, "This is my Son whom I dearly love; I find happiness in him." Then scripture says that immediately after his baptism, Jesus was led into the desert by the Spirit to be tempted by the Scratcher. A test to see if there were any job stoppers.

Once again, the Scratcher went with the tried-and-true lies: lies about our true Artist, lies about ourselves, and lies about the world around us.

The first test Satan threw at Jesus was this: "If you are the Son of God, tell these stones to become bread." *If you are the Son of God.* This was not about getting Jesus to doubt who he was. This was a test of "How are you going to act now, in light of the fact of who you are?"

After fasting for forty days and nights, Jesus was hungry. He could have easily used his power to turn stones to bread. But for him to be our perfect Savior, he would have to experience fully what it means to be human. If Jesus was going to save us, he couldn't save himself. He refused. He would trust that God would provide for him.

For the next test, the Scratcher led Jesus to Jerusalem, to stand on the highest point of the temple. "Since you are God's Son, throw yourself down; for it is written, *I will command my angels concerning you, and they will take you up in their hands so that you won't hit your foot on a stone.*" The first test proved that Jesus was a man with faith in God. This test proved just how much faith he had.

As our friend Ellen said, "Throw yourself off a high building just so God can save you? God already *did* save you. You don't need to prove yourself to God. He loves you as you are, He sees you as you are, He created you and He knows you. Don't put yourself in negative situations just for God to save you—He already did."

Again, Jesus resisted.

Last, the Scratcher led Jesus to a very high mountain and showed him all the glory of the kingdoms of the world. "I'll give you all these," the Scratcher said, "if you bow down and worship me." This last test was about power.

It was a tempting offer. Jesus might have still been able to accomplish a lot in the name of righteousness, but he remembered that he had a higher purpose. He wasn't looking to rule the existing kingdoms. He reigns in a new kingdom—a new heaven and a new earth. His eye is on the spiritual, not the physical. A third time, he resisted the poisonous ink.

F. L. Anderson wrote,

> In each case the appeal was a real appeal to a perfectly innocent natural instinct or appetite. In the first temptation, it was to hunger; in the second, to faith; in the third, to power as a means of establishing righteousness. In each case, Jesus felt the tug and pull of the natural instinct. . . . Yet, when He perceived that the satisfaction of these desires was sinful under the conditions, He immediately refused their clamorous appeal. It was a glorious moral victory. . . . Only the victor can help the vanquished; only he, who has felt the most dreadful assaults and yet has stood firm, can give the help needed by the fallen.

That's us. The fallen. The apostle Peter wrote that "he himself bore our sins in his body on the cross, so that we might die to sins and live for righteousness." The Scratcher can't lay claim on those who belong to Christ, but he still slings the toxic ink—lies about our true Artist, lies about ourselves, and lies about the world

around us—to try to rob us of our life's purpose to be showcases for the Master Artist.

It seems everywhere we look, he's trying to etch into our minds doubts about God—that He exists, that He is good, that He is faithful. That He loves us. That He deserves our complete devotion. The Scratcher throws job stoppers left and right. Job stoppers we choose to ignore in favor of better ink.

When religious leaders thought Jesus was just a demon-possessed man, he responded by telling them they were listening to the devil, the father of lies—the one who has forever been trying to cast doubt about Christ's identity. He said to them, "Very truly I tell you . . . before Abraham was born, I am!" His use of the very name God used in identifying himself to Moses was his way of saying that he is the son of God and preexisted Abraham. "'I am the Alpha and the Omega,' says the Lord God, 'the one who is and was and is coming, the Almighty.'" In other words, you can't stain me with your toxic ink because I am truth and everything in me is truth. You don't tattoo my identity, because I am the Master Artist.

Our master artist.

The Scratcher attempts to mark us with doubt: of Jesus' love for us, of our position as children of God, of our worth. And too often, we buy into it. We question how we can make a difference in this world. We worry that we're too messed up, we don't deserve happiness. That things will never change. The Scratcher comes to steal, kill, and destroy. But Jesus Christ came to give us abundant life.

Lies about our Master Artist, about ourselves, and about the world around us permeate our culture. See if you recognize any of these lies from your own life:

1. *All-or-Nothing Thinking.* You tend to deal only in absolutes; everything is either black or white, no gray areas. In tattoo-world, think Kat Von D, owner of High Voltage Tattoo, or rapper Lil Wayne with serious coverage of ink. No tentative little dragonfly on the ankle. For them, it's all or nothing.
2. *Emotional Reasoning.* Geena Davis had to have her tat of her ex-husband's name altered to look like a Denny's restaurant logo, and Pamela Anderson had to convert the "T" in the inked "Tommy" around her ring finger to an "M" after divorcing rocker Tommy Lee. Like one who permanently marks her body believing her love is eternal, emotional reasoning is when you let your emotions cloud your good judgment.
3. *Overgeneralization.* Speaking of Tommy Lee, he has "Mayhem" inked across his abdomen in big Old English letters. If it were more than just homage to the band he cofounded, Methods of Mayhem, you might say he was overgeneralizing—defining himself or the world around him based on one negative event, resigned to an endless pattern of defeat.
4. *Labeling.* Let's be honest. Most of us have probably passed a fully tatted guy on the street and assumed he was a gang member, an ex-con, or a drug user. That's called labeling, or

jumping to conclusions. And if that guy was Bruce Potts, we'd be wrong. Bruce has a full and very colorful tribal tattoo that covers his entire face and head . . . and he's a respected retired teacher from the University of New Mexico.

5. *Shoulds.* Kathryn Schulz, journalist and author of *Being Wrong: Adventures in the Margin of Error*, illustrates her ideas about living with regrets by revealing her own tattoo in a video presentation. We won't give it away in case you'd like to watch it yourself, but she leaves her audience with this statement: "We need to learn to love the flawed, imperfect things that we create and to forgive ourselves for creating them." One artist told us that if he can tell a potential client is prone to perfectionism, he'll refuse to do their tattoo rather than risk that they would disparage his reputation. Yes, we are flawed and imperfect, but our Artist has called us a masterpiece made in his own image.
6. *Disqualifying the Positive.* Angelina Jolie used to have a small window tattooed on her lower back (it's now covered by the tail of her Bengal tiger tattoo). While she said she's no longer stained by this view on life, the window used to refer to the fact that, wherever she was, she found herself "looking out the window, wishing I was somewhere else." *Really?* Hard to imagine Angelina Jolie—Academy Award winner, three-time Golden Globe award winner, twice named by *Forbes* as the highest paid actress in Hollywood, voted most beautiful woman in the world by *Vanity Fair* readers, humanitarian and goodwill ambassador, founder of several

charitable organizations, mother of six, and romantic partner to Brad Pitt—ever wishing she were somewhere else. When we reject affirming experiences, counting them for nothing, it's called *disqualifying the positive*.

7. *Mental Filter.* Recording artist Rihanna grew up with an abusive and drug-addicted father. Rihanna reports that she became a loner through the experience, bottling up her emotions. Years later, on the night before the 2009 Grammys, then-boyfriend Chris Brown punched her and choked her until she nearly passed out, then left her in his car on the side of the road, her face bloody and swollen.

Later, Rihanna told *Rolling Stone*, "I put my guard up so hard. I didn't want people to see me cry. I didn't want people to feel bad for me. It was a very vulnerable time in my life, and I refused to let that be the image. I wanted them to see me as, 'I'm fine, I'm tough.' I put that up until it felt real." In the months that followed the incident, she would also have a small handgun inked a few inches below her right armpit. Her tattoo artist, Keith "Bang Bang" McCurdy, said it's a symbol of "strength and power."

We wonder if it's a mental filter from her experiences. Dr. David Burns describes a mental filter like this: "You pick out a single negative detail and dwell on it exclusively so that your vision of all reality becomes narrow as though you have blinders on." Rihanna has a tattoo on

her opposite rib cage, a phrase tattooed in Arabic that truly describes strength and power. *That* tattoo says "Freedom in Christ."

8. *Magnification or Minimization*. On the other hand, Rihanna's thirteenth tattoo is her life motto inked on her chest, tattooed backward so she can read it in a mirror: "Never a failure, always a lesson." According to Dr. Burns, based on this tattoo, Rihanna doesn't have a problem with magnification or minimization, which is "when you exaggerate the importance of things (such as your goof-up, or someone else's achievement), or you inappropriately shrink things until they appear tiny (your own desirable qualities or the other fellow's imperfections)." It doesn't matter if you think you're a grasshopper if God sees you as a mighty warrior.
9. *Personalization*. According to several websites, one of the most common tattoos is the anchor—representing safety, salvation, and hope. The caption that often accompanies the picture on these websites reads, "In a world that's chaotic and violent, who wouldn't want such refuge?" Only one Anchor represents our safety, salvation, and hope. If you find yourself trying to control a situation over which you have no power, let go and find refuge in the anchor described by the writer of Hebrews: "We have this hope as an anchor for the soul, firm and secure."

Combating the Scratcher

There's a force that seeks to chisel lies into our thinking, and his list of tactics goes on and on. In addition to the poison ink already described, we could add the need to win other people's approval, anxiety, busy social calendars, and materialism, as well as all kinds of flash and the distractions that vie for our attention. But there's a way to combat the Scratcher.

Long before Katy Perry ever thought of getting a Jesus tattoo on her wrist to always remind her where her roots began, God commanded his people to tie symbolic reminders of his commandments on their wrists and foreheads. Even then, people were unable to stick to the six hundred–plus laws of the old covenant (which were really symbolic in pointing them to Jesus), so God provided a new covenant, a way to know their true Artist. This time, God said He would imprint His law onto their minds and write it on their hearts. And what ink machine did God use? Jesus.

One heavily tattooed attorney said, "The relationship between the person getting the tattoo and the artist is almost like an intimacy. You're allowing someone to penetrate you with a needle, and you're trusting them to do it right." To resist the Scratcher, we need to be intimate with Scripture, which is really intimacy with Christ. When the apostle Paul wrote about how to resist the gashes of the Scratcher, he told us to pick up the sword of the Spirit, which is the Word of God. In order to develop immunity against the Scratcher's toxic ink, we need the truth of the word ingrained on our minds.

Jesus responded to each of the Scratcher's tactics with the truth. Which means that if we tend to reason with our emotions, He'll tell us to "guard your heart above everything else, because it determines the course of your life." If we tend to disqualify the positive, Jesus will remind us that we can do everything through him who gives us strength. If we struggle with perfectionism, he'll remind us that we all have different gifts, according to the grace given us.

Josh Hamilton told us that resisting the Scratcher's toxins with Scripture was critical to his comeback:

> Any thought that lasts for eight seconds can become an obsession and then a reality. That's what happened in the past. I'd think about it until it became a reality and would drink or use. It was the hardest thing to overcome. When I got sober for real, I learned to replace the bad thoughts with scripture. You can't think about two thoughts at the same time. That became the turning point in my life and recovery.

Like antibodies to the Scratcher's poison ink, the Word reminds us of the tattoo-worthy.

Besides developing an intimacy with Scripture in order to resist the Scratcher's needles, Jesus also told his disciples to pray. Since we're already covered by serious ink—our choice to accept Jesus as our Master Artist—we can approach God's throne with confidence. We know that we have God's ear and that Jesus sits at God's right hand and talks with Him about us.

John Reardon wrote, "Tattoo equipment is very sacred to a tattooist. The tools the tattooist uses determine how well the tattoo will turn out." The apostle Paul wrote that our sacred tools, prayer and scripture, are powered by God to demolish the strongholds in our lives. Prayer and the Scripture, Paul wrote, are the tools we use to take our thoughts captive and to line them up with Christ.

Tattooist Guy Aitchison wrote, "Working with as little power as you can get away with can leave you with too little punch for the job," and adds this advice for tattoo artists: "Don't be afraid to use power when necessary." How much we use God's word and prayer will determine how well our tattoos turn out—tattoos that, as the apostle Paul wrote, are "written not with ink but with the Spirit of the living God, not on tablets of stone but on tablets of human hearts."

From Gashes to Glory

Pete will tell you that God had been trying to make an impression on him his whole life. When, at twelve years old, he was caught breaking into the Christian center in his neighborhood and tearing the strings out of the piano, his "punishment" was being sent to a church camp for ten days. His face lit up when he described the campfires, the hikes and teepees, and the churched kids who didn't know quite what to make of him. "I loved it!" he exclaimed. So much so that, sometime later, he threatened to damage something again so that he could be sent back. The preacher told him he didn't need to destroy any more property—they'd send him to camp. Pete said, "In all my growing up, those were the best twenty days of my life."

But that early ink didn't permeate totally or immediately. Pete ended up joining a biker gang in the sixties and said he didn't have anything more to do with God until his grandmother died in 1999. Ashamed, he admitted he didn't have a family minister to preach her funeral, so the funeral director offered a list of local ministers. As God would have it, one of the ministers on the list was the former president of a rival biker gang. Since his own dramatic conversion, he had become a minister and started a Christian motorcycle club. Instead of financial payment, the outlaw-turned-minister agreed to preach Pete's grandmother's funeral with one condition: Pete would go to church just one time. Pete agreed, and when he fulfilled his part of the bargain (a full year later), he found God waiting for him. He's been permanently inked by Christ ever since.

After his transformation, every time he looked at his tattoo from his upside-down vantage point, Pete said that it grated on him that MAD DOG resembled something profane and blasphemous. While sitting in a welding shop one day, he happened to mention this to his tattoo artist friend. As it happened, the friend had his machines and ink in the car. Right there in the welding shop, his friend covered over the reminder of Pete's past life with a tribute to his new life. A rugged cross completely covers the old lettering and, above it, new letters form the words SAVED BY CHRIST.

His old identity is covered by the cross, quite literally.

Lilly also decided to cover over the hack marks of her own self-appointed identity. The new image, a tiger lily, matches the nickname given to her as a little girl, a time that reminds her of innocence and hope. Symbolic to her that God does bring beauty out of ashes, she now uses her mark to speak to young women about their identity in Christ.

Pete and Lilly have been grazed by the Scratcher, but their Artist turned it around.

The idea that we can be new creations in Christ isn't just a church concept anymore. It's gaining significant support in scientific circles. It's even given birth to a new field called neurotheology—the study of how religious and spiritual experiences change the brain. Dr. Andrew Newberg, a pioneer in neurotheology and coauthor of *How God Changes Your Brain: Breakthrough Findings from a Leading Neuroscientist*, wrote, "Our research team at the University of Pennsylvania has consistently demonstrated that God is part of our consciousness and that the more you think about God, the more you will alter the neural circuitry in specific parts of your brain. That is why I say, with the utmost confidence, that God can change your brain."

The Scratcher's lies are designed to steal our purpose, to kill our relationship with our Artist, and to destroy our lives. But God can change our brains—the way we think. God can turn our gashes into glory.

Engrave It!

1. What tainted ink has the Scratcher hacked into your mind—about your Artist, about yourself, or about the world around you? Take some time to think about it and write it down. Next, search for Scripture that takes each contaminated mark captive and write it down. Memorize the truth. Each time a toxic thought pops into your mind, say the Scripture out loud.
2. Take the most toxic thought from the list above, the one that has been a job stopper for you, rendering you less than what your Artist created you to be. Imagine what you would tattoo on your body as a representation of that thought. Now, picture Christ going to the cross for you to destroy the Scratcher's mark and to grant you access to the throne of God. Meditate on the fact that when God looks at you, He sees the blood of Christ sprinkled over the old tattoo. Thank God for this indescribable gift, and ask God to help you resist the Scratcher's needle in the future.

B-Backs and Wrastlers: Getting (and Staying) in the Chair

Your name will no longer be Jacob, but Israel,

because you have struggled with God and

with men and have overcome.

—Genesis 32:28 (NIV)

To become a freak one needs a strong character and unusual determination.

—George Burchett, Memoirs of a Tattooist

On Labor Day weekend in 2008, Janet's longtime friend from high school, Cathy Grudowski, was vacationing with her husband, Dave, in Casey Key, Florida. They met a ranger who invited them to join her before sunup the next morning to help excavate three loggerhead turtle nests. Three days before, the ranger had marked that the eggs had hatched; now it was time to make sure all of the babies got out of the nests. Although Cathy wasn't thrilled about getting up before dawn to do it, she said in retrospect that saying no would have meant missing out on one of the most vivid spiritual tattoos of her life.

They found seven baby loggerheads, each only about two inches in diameter, either caught in the roots or simply too weak to make it out. One had damaged his flipper in the struggle to dig himself out and was taken to the Mote Aquarium nursery for rehab. Later he was released in the weed bed about four miles out in the Gulf to join his siblings. In an amazing mark of perseverance, the babies stay in that weed bed until they are big enough to survive in the open ocean. Eventually the females return to the same beach where they were hatched and lay their own eggs.

Cathy said that in her fifty-something years of knowing her Artist, she has never felt his steady hand quite the way she did that morning as she held, named, and helped God's helpless creatures. In the year ahead, she would need God's steady hand as her life would be inked by an even deeper mark.

Little did the Grudowskis know when they were helping the baby loggerheads survive that Dave had cancer and would die a little more than a year later. Cathy placed his ashes in the very spot where he asked her to—in the loggerheads' weed bed. She still feels the sting of the mark his death has left on her, but she knows that Dave's perseverance in his faith means that ultimately death has lost its sting and that he has eternal life. To mark her love for Dave and her belief in that fact, Cathy immediately got a henna tattoo and is working up the nerve to make it permanent: near her right ankle, a tiny baby loggerhead turtle, looking just the way they do when they hatch.

Where the Needle Meets the Skin

Once we've chosen our artist and have decided to be inked with the tattoo worthy, it's time for that fateful moment. No more putting it off, no more excuses. It's time to get in the chair. This is where the needle meets skin. We could, of course, still back out at this point. We'd be what they call in the business a B-Back—

someone who chickens out and says something like, "I'll be back; I've gotta get something to eat first," never to be seen again.

That moment comes for all of us. That moment where we have to decide just how much we really believe in our Artist, and just how much we're willing to be permanently inked by him.

For a certain young man, the moment of decision came when he approached Jesus with this question: "Good Teacher, what must I do to obtain eternal life?" Jesus asked, "Why do you call me good? No one is good except the one God." Then he said to the young man, "You know the commandments. Don't commit murder. Don't commit adultery. Don't steal. Don't give false testimony. Don't cheat. Honor your father and mother." When the man replied that he had kept these commandments since he was a boy, Jesus told him there was one thing he lacked: "Go, sell what you own, and give the money to the poor. Then you will have treasure in heaven. And come, follow me." The Gospel of Mark records that the man's face fell and he walked away. The cost was too great. He had already been too deeply marked by affluence and couldn't get in the chair.

Jesus' request to the young man might seem harsh. After all, it's not a sin to be rich, right? King David was rich, and God called him a man after his own heart. But here's where the apostle Mark says something in his account of the story that's easy to gloss over: "Jesus looked at him carefully and loved him."

The Artist carefully looks over all the marks that have been made on the canvas of our lives, and he loves us anyway. He may never ask us to sell everything we have, but he does ask, "Are you willing to let go of the smears and smudges that have stained you and let me make a more vivid design of your life?"

Setting Your Hope Fully

Any reputable tattooist will insist that you're sober when you get in his chair, and our Artist is no exception. The apostle Peter wrote, "With minds that are alert and fully sober," then he focused on the reward for getting in the chair: "set your hope on the grace to be brought to you when Jesus Christ is revealed at his coming." Getting in the chair means we're ready to commit our priorities and purpose to his design for our lives. It's time to allow God to ink on us what He will. The ultimate design will be worth getting in the chair, no matter the cost.

Cathy Grudowski describes that morning of saving the seven baby loggerheads as one where she felt the hovering presence of her Artist more intensely than in her whole life, and that morning made such a deep mark on Dave that he wanted his ashes placed in the weed bed where the sea turtles were launched into their freedom. Why? Because at that moment, they both felt part of a design that was much bigger than themselves.

How do we discover the Artist's design for our lives? By spending time with God in prayer, hearing from Him through the written word, listening to what others see in us, taking time to discover our spiritual gifts and talents, and paying attention to what gets our hearts beating. And visualizing our design, concentrating

on the end result, down to every stroke of the needle. When we do, we create mental images that form the basis for our thoughts, and those thoughts affect our reality.

After Josh Hamilton was drafted, every time he saw Coach Clay Council, the man who had been devoted to helping young baseball players when Josh was growing up in North Carolina, Josh would say that if he were ever in the Home Run Derby, he wanted Coach Council to throw to him. And when Josh Hamilton, the B-Back who actually did come back and actually did find himself hitting at the Home Run Derby on that now famous night of July 14, 2008, who do you think was throwing to him? Seventy-one-year-old Clay Council.

Our friend Carter's dad relayed this story over breakfast one morning. Carter's mom and dad were visiting his third-grade classroom. Sitting in the little chairs, they listened as Carter read a story he had written about a little boy who went to a go-kart racing school. His dad paused in his retelling of the story and asked Carter (who was taking a bite of chocolate chip pancake), "And did you know anything about go-kart school before writing the story?" Carter smiled, shook his head, and said, "Nope." His dad asked, "Had you ever heard about go-kart school, or seen a commercial about it on TV?" Again Carter smiled and shook his head no.

Sitting in that classroom and listening to him read his story, Carter's parents were flabbergasted. His birthday was in two days, and they had bought him go-kart lessons! Not only did Carter have no idea, but he hadn't even asked for go-kart lessons. Carter even ended up winning two out of the three races at the end of the classes, just like the boy in his story! (Carter was quick to explain that he lost the one race only because there was something wrong with his car.) His dad joked that he was going to write a story about a man who wakes up one morning and finds a big trash bag full of unmarked bills on his front porch!

When we visualize our design, we actively partner with our Artist in inking a new, more brilliant pattern. In *Man's Search for Meaning*, Viktor Frankl wrote that any effort to fight the prison camp's mental effects on a prisoner had to involve getting a vision of a future design on his life. He tells of two different men who were thinking of getting out of the chair permanently—by committing suicide:

> Both used the typical argument—they had nothing more to expect from life. In both cases it was a question of getting them to realize that life was still expecting something from them: something in the future was expected of them. We found, in fact, that for the one it was his child whom he adored and who was waiting for him in a foreign country. For the other it was a thing, not a person. This man was a scientist and had written a series of books which still needed to be finished. His work could not be done by anyone else, any more than another person could ever take the place of the father in his child's affections. . . . When the impossibility of replacing a person is realized, it allows the responsibility which a man has for his existence and its continuance to appear in all its magnitude. A man who becomes conscious of the responsibility he bears toward a human being who affectionately waits for him, or to an unfinished work, will never be able to throw away his life.

When Frankl himself grew tired of the monotonous thoughts of survival, he visualized his own future design: "Suddenly I saw myself standing on the platform of a well-lit, warm and pleasant lecture room. In front of me sat an attentive audience on comfortable upholstered seats. I was giving a lecture on the psychology of the concentration camp!" Of course, in actuality, he would find himself, postliberation, lecturing all over the world about what the marks of the concentration camp had taught him about the meaning of life.

Visualizing your design is powerful. Josh Hamilton and Carter would tell us it helps us realize our dreams. Viktor Frankl would tell us it's a matter of physical life and death. The apostle Paul would tell us it is of eternal importance. And your Artist has a custom design for you.

Wrastling with God

Sometimes after deciding to get in the chair, we struggle with staying in the chair. We've committed to Christ and his purposes for us, but life gets hard. Staying in the chair hurts. We get weary. At this point, some are tempted to give up. But some push through the pain and the exhaustion. These are the ones tattoo artists call "wrastlers"—people who, even after fainting in the chair, still decide to finish what they started.

Genesis 32 paints a beautiful picture of what it means to "wrastle" with God. It seemed Jacob's whole life was marked by wrastling. From the womb, he was grabbing the heel of his twin brother, Esau. Later, he wrastled Esau's blessing from their father, although, as the firstborn son, it was rightfully Esau's. Furious, Esau planned to kill Jacob for taking his blessing, so Jacob ran away from home. In that new land, he wrastled a man named Laban for fourteen years in order to marry Laban's two daughters, Rachel and Leah.

Tired of wrastling with his father-in-law for so long, Jacob decided to return to his homeland of Canaan. On his way, messengers told him that Esau was coming in his direction with four hundred men. Even though twenty years had passed since he had seen his brother, Jacob was used to a lifetime of wrastling and had every reason to expect that his brother still wanted to kill him. But in all his years of wrastling, the Bible records that Jacob had stayed in the chair—he had maintained a relationship with his Artist.

The night before Jacob was to cross back over the Jordan, he talked with his Artist. God told Jacob that He was the same Artist who had marked the lives of Jacob's father, Isaac, and his grandfather Abraham; the same Artist who had been kind and faithful toward him when he had first crossed the Jordan River some twenty years ago; and the same Artist who told him to go back to his relatives. And Jacob asked his Artist to save him and his family from Esau.

All alone, on the night before he was to face his brother and four hundred men, having no reason to believe that his brother didn't still want to kill him, Jacob, who had always taken matters into his own hands, was at the end of himself. No amount of deception and no amount of material wealth could help him.

That's when God came in the form of a man and wrestled with Jacob. In fact, they wrestled until dawn, until, realizing that Jacob would not give up, God touched the socket of Jacob's hip so that it was displaced. Obviously, God could have defeated Jacob had he wanted to, but he had planned a design for Jacob's life and it was more important that God stay within the lines of that design rather than beat Jacob in a wrestling match.

So the Artist "touched" Jacob, to show him what God could do and whom Jacob was really wrestling with. Our modern translations lead us to imagine a gentle touch, but the original Hebrew can also mean "strike," as in a more violent blow. However gentle a touch or violent a blow, we know it marked Jacob for the rest of his life.

Regardless, Jacob continued wrestling even after his hip had been dislocated, until God finally told him to let go, because it was daybreak. But Jacob replied, "I will not let you go unless you bless me."

Jacob had been self-reliant and independent his whole life. But the prophet Hosea clues us in to something about this exchange that isn't mentioned in Genesis. He adds that Jacob "wept and begged for his favor." Jacob was hanging on, weeping and pleading, "I will not let you go unless you bless me."

The Artist looked down on Jacob with a look of love as He held him up. God asked Jacob, "What is your name?"

"Jacob."

"Your name will no longer be Jacob, but Israel, because you have struggled with God and with humans and have overcome." Then God blessed him. And Jacob limped toward his homeland.

Where do we "wrastle" with our Artist? What tempts us to get out of the chair? We've all had times in our lives where we've had to persevere, even if it left us limping for a time. Our friend Monica has. She's had to demonstrate perseverance unlike that of almost anyone we know. And, like Jacob, after wrestling with God, she has been able to say that God has answered her whenever she was in trouble and has been with her wherever she's gone. Rather than tell you her story, we'll let her tell it to you:

> At the age of 8, I went to visit Grandma. Any time spent with her was precious now that she was 6 hours from us as a result of a recent move. She was a unique jewel in every way and I would have gone with her anywhere if it meant being together. So when she mentioned going to her church for the evening, I was game as it was extra time with Grandma.
>
> What was to follow would change my life forever. Had I only known, I would have perhaps worn something more sophisticated to commemorate the moment. In my blue jeans and T-shirt, complete with little-girl braids in my hair, I accepted the Lord as my Savior; and true to His character, He accepted me—just as I was.

As a human race, we blew it. As a loving Father, He made up for it. Simple message, huge impact. No social injustice, no offense, can ever compare to what He did for us and we need only believe on Him (John 3:36). His promise that night was that He would never leave me nor forsake me . . . and He has always been true to that promise:

By age 15 I lost my father to suicide and subsequently dropped out of high school. But He said:

"I will never leave you nor forsake you" (Hebrews 13:5).

By age 17 I was on my 6th stepfather, but He said:

"I will never leave you nor forsake you."

By age 19 I had my identity stolen by my mother, whom I had idolized to this point, resulting in thousands in debt, taking years to pay off and leaving exactly 1 penny left per paycheck every week, but He said:

"I will never leave you nor forsake you."

By age 20 I had serious pre-cancerous issues, but He said:

"I will never leave you nor forsake you."

By age 22 I took 2 years of high school and the $40 to my name and went to college without a clue as to where to start, and the Lord said:

"I will never leave you nor forsake you."

By age 30 I had the pleasure of caring for Mom on her deathbed, patching our relationship up before losing her, and He said:

"I will never leave you nor forsake you."

At age 31 I spent my birthday burying my (previously mentioned) dear Grandmother, and He said:

"I will never leave you nor forsake you."

By age 35 I said good-bye to my brother/best friend as he went for vacation in Colorado, only to die in his sleep after a long hike, and the Lord said:

"I will never leave you nor forsake you."

By age 37 I lost my nephew suddenly, but the Lord said:

"I will never leave you nor forsake you."

By age 39 I lost another nephew unexpectedly and had to tell his mother (my sister) on Mother's Day that her only remaining son was gone forever, but the Lord said:

"I will never leave you nor forsake you."

At age 40 I was given a golden job opportunity and plans were delayed due to unexpected skin cancer, but He said:

"I will never leave you nor forsake you."

Lord, thank you for all you've seen me through, but I still have some deep concerns. Terrorism is on the rise, the stock market is the worst it's been in my lifetime, the doctors are giving me personal statistics that are far from comforting, I'm going to a foreign country alone, and, and, and . . .

"Monica."

Yes, Lord?

"I said never."

Deciding to hang in there with your Artist is not for the faint of heart. We don't know what that moment will be for you, but we all have them—moments where we're faced with whether to continue being inked by the same Artist or to get out of the chair. For Cathy Grudowski, one of those moments was losing Dave, her life partner and love of her life, to cancer. She's experienced loneliness, fear, and sadness. She's wondered if she'll ever stop crying. But she decided to stay in the chair.

For the apostle Paul, one of those moments was when the people of Lystra stoned him, dragged him outside the city, and left him for dead. But, to his friends' amazement, Paul got back up and went right back into the city! He got right back in the chair. Years later, he would write about his serious commitment: "I forget about the things behind me and reach out for the things ahead of me. The goal I pursue is the prize of God's upward call in Christ Jesus."

In *The Complete Idiot's Guide to Getting a Tattoo*, John Reardon wrote, "To become heavily tattooed with large pieces, you must be prepared to commit yourself to getting your work completed." God honors our "wrastling." God *wants* us to have the kind of persevering faith that says, "I won't let go until you bless me!" But God also wants us to rest in Him, to rest from the marks of sin and strife and instead find rest in the complete fulfillment of the design God has for us.

The writer of Hebrews helps us understand where we find our rest: "Therefore, brothers and sisters who are partners in the heavenly calling"—because of all of this, because he became like you in every way so that he can help you when you are tempted, because he got in the chair and stayed in the chair—"think about Jesus." The New International Version says "fix your thoughts on Jesus."

Jesus had to be made like his brothers in every way. What's your biggest temptation? Jesus faced it. Are you tempted to get out of the chair? So was Jesus. Whatever temptation we can name, Jesus was tempted by the same thing.

He wrastled with God harder than we have ever thought about. When he was tempted, he faced the full unleashing of the temptation, long past any point where you or I would have caved. And when Jesus had completed all he was sent to do on earth, Luke records that "he steadfastly set his face to go to Jerusalem." One commentator said he "firmly determined to accomplish his design."

Because the Artist was so intently focused on our design, the work is done. Our rest is found in God. The writer of Hebrews says to "fix our eyes on Jesus, faith's pioneer and perfecter. He endured the cross, ignoring the shame, for the sake of the joy that was laid out in front of him, and sat down at the right side of God's throne." He sits at the right hand of the throne of God to intercede for us when we are wrastling in the chair. Because he got in the chair and stayed in the chair, he's able to help us stay in the chair. More than that, he's the Artist who gets in the chair with us. So, let's fix our eyes on him.

Those who hope in the LORD *will renew their strength.*
They will soar on wings like eagles; they will run and
not grow weary, they will walk and not be faint.
—Isaiah 40:31 (NIV)

Engrave It!

1. In the same way that Monica took an inventory of her marks, think about the marks that have been made on your own life. When have you "wrastled" to stay in the chair? How was your relationship with your Artist impacted? What lessons did you learn from the marks? How might your Artist be using those marks to design God's purpose on your life?
2. Is there a goal or design that God has put on your heart? Perhaps it's covering over the marks of an old habit, or maybe it's to create a new habit. Practice these steps for visualizing your achievement of the new design.
   a. Sit in a comfortable position.
   b. Relax by breathing slowly.
   c. Picture yourself accomplishing the goal. If it is a behavior you want to stop, picture a scene where the problem occurs, then replay the scene—only this time, picture yourself accomplishing the behavior that you want to accomplish.
   d. Tell yourself positive statements: "This will get easier," "I am achieving my ultimate design," and so forth. Each time you picture your new design, you impact your ability to achieve it.
3. Draw seven circles to represent each day of the week. For the next week, using different colors or shadings, fill in the pie-shaped increments to chart how you spend your time during

each day (school, work, sleeping, time with God, volunteering, socializing, watching TV, working out). Chart everything. Ask yourself: Is the reality of where I spend my time leading toward the ultimate design the Artist has on my life? What ink is bleeding outside the lines of my intended design? What do I need to eliminate so that my reality begins to morph into that design? What color is lacking from the ultimate design?

Kickin' It into Third: Achieving the Desired Result

Rejoice always. Pray continually.

Give thanks in every situation because this is God's

will for you in Christ Jesus.

—1 Thessalonians 5:16-18

A speedier machine will also be set as to the thickness or the condition of your customer's skin. If he has got thick tough skin then you are obviously going to have to turn your machine up a bit in order to puncture that skin.

—Chip Taylor, Tattooist

Life's struggles and marks can give us pretty thick skin. We may have chosen our Artist a long time ago, but if we've been in His chair for a while, we can get less sensitive to the power of the machines. We lose our excitement for His design on our lives.

Once Lilly got a vision of God's design for her, she had the self-inflicted "WHORE" on her thigh filled in with a beautiful tiger lily. She got in God's chair and allowed Him to fill in the marks of her shame and low self-esteem, and she's been in God's chair ever since. But that doesn't mean that her struggle with anxiety about the future and figuring out her identity instantly went away.

She would still wrastle with God, especially when she moved to a new city, married, got a new job, and went back to finish college—all in the same year. She would worry about being a good wife, making good grades, managing finances, preparing to start a family, and planning for the future. Sure, she was in her Artist's chair, but she was numb to God's work.

Looking back on it now, she can see how God was still there and doing His work. One week after she graduated, she called Kim. "How would you like to do some research for the tattoo book and provide me some moral support at the same time?" As a graduation present to herself, she had decided to ink between her shoulder blades the Scripture that was her touchstone during that season.

A few days later, Kim found herself at Metamorphosis (voted the number one tattoo and piercing shop in Indianapolis), furiously chewing peppermint gum to avoid passing out from the aroma of isopropyl alcohol in the air, the grinding of the machines, and the sight of a stranger piercing her dear friend's exposed back. It didn't help that hanging on the wall was a piece of antique tattoo equipment that looked like a prop right out of *Saw V*. Kim popped another piece of gum and made idle chatter in an effort to distract Lilly from the pain.

It turns out that scar tissue is more delicate than normal skin and therefore more painful as a tattoo surface. The tattooist uses a slower speed on the machine and may have to go over the area multiple times in order to get the scarred skin to take the ink.

Getting her tiger lily tattoo had taken more than two incredibly painful hours, so Kim and Lilly were both surprised when the tattooist turned off the machine and handed Lilly a mirror just half an hour after he'd started. The words from the pattern she had handed to the artist only a few minutes before were now permanently stamped on her back:

> *Blessed be the Lord, who hath not*
> *given us as a prey to their teeth.*
> *Our soul is escaped as a bird out*
> *of the snare of the fowlers:*
> *the snare is broken, and we are escaped.*
> *Our help is in the name of the Lord,*
> *who made heaven and earth.*
> *Psalm 124:6 -8*

It's true of us too. After the Scratcher has done his damage, we often have to learn the truth over and over before it finally settles in.

When Lilly got her first tattoo, she'd learned that God brings glory out of gashes. But between then and now, life had caused her to lose sight of the God she worships—the one who made heaven and earth and who could surely handle her problems.

"Kickin' it into third" is tattoo slang for when the artist picks up the speed on the ink fill because he knows you can handle it. Like tattooist Chip Taylor said at the beginning of this chapter, thicker skin requires a faster speed. Lilly had long been a Christian. She'd long ago chosen her tattooist, chosen custom work over flash, and learned how to combat the Scratcher. She'd decided to get in the chair and stay in the chair. But having developed some thick skin since then, it was time to kick it into third.

Like many of us, Lilly struggles with what Dr. George Lincoln Walton, consulting neurologist to the Massachusetts General Hospital, called in 1908 "the disease of our age"—worry. Things haven't changed much in more than a hundred years. Nine out of ten of the most prescribed psychiatric drugs in America in 2010 were anxiety medications, accounting for more than two hundred million prescriptions.

We recently polled a group of students about what worries them most. The top reason was "the future," with its close runner-up, "not measuring up." It seems we're all worked up over some indefinable expectations. We may not have the vaguest notion of what we expect for ourselves, but we cringe at the thought of not meeting others' expectations, most of all God's.

So many of our prayers include a plea for God to reveal His design for our lives—what education we should obtain, what career to pursue, whom to marry, where to live. Our friend Jack Schmit has a master's degree in counseling, a doctorate in college administration, has cowritten a book on how students make decisions regarding their futures, and has spent fifteen years working with students from middle school to graduate school in college-access programs. He's built a career out of helping people figure out what to do with their lives. Years ago during a phone conversation, listening to Kim fret about seeking God's will for her life, he said, "All right, Kim, do you want to know God's will for your life?"

"*Yes*, Jack, I want to know God's will for my life! That's what I've been telling you!"

"Get your Bible."

She grabbed a Bible. "Got it."

"Okay, turn to 1 Thessalonians 5:16-18."

"Got it."

"Read it to me."

"Be joyful always; pray continually; give thanks in all circumstances, for this is God's will for you in Christ Jesus."

For this is God's will for you. Well, there it is. In black and white. No more excuses. No more procrastination.

We often get caught up in the nitty-gritty, demanding that God give us the details. But God has already drawn the outline. He gives us a lot of freedom in choosing the colors and shadings, but He's already given us the big-picture design.

Be joyful always.

Pray continually.

Give thanks in all circumstances.

There it is—the trifecta of God's will for us. Follow His promise to us, seek His kingdom, and everything else will be taken care of.

When Paul wrote, "Don't be conformed to the patterns of this world, but be transformed by the renewing of your minds so that you can figure out what God's will is," he called that will "good and pleasing and mature." The Greek for "will" is *theléma*, and it means God's desire, the result God hopes for, His "best offer."

God's offer is better than what the world has to offer, and it's time to kick it into third. When we practice these three commands—when we can handle picking up the speed on the fill—the details will emerge.

Be Joyful Always

On the surface, always being joyful seems like a tall order. Because life's pressures threaten to steal our joy. And the people around us don't always cooperate with our joyful attitude. We may wake up with a song in our hearts, but our families, roommates, or coworkers may not share our enthusiasm.

People and pressures make it tough to be joyful always, but Kim once had an experience that squelched all her excuses for not being joyful:

> *For months, I had been going through one of the darkest times of my life. It was all I could do to pray, "Help, God. Just show me you love me." That was all that seemed to matter at the time. One particular Sunday morning, I added, "God, don't let the pain I've gone through be for nothing. Use it. Don't let me be just an empty shell on this earth for the rest of my days, but help me to be joyful and live life abundantly again."*

Later, running late into church, I slid into a pew behind a mother with her son who looked to be around seven or eight. I soon realized the boy was deaf when his mother started signing to him and that he was otherwise physically disabled because his wheelchair was parked in the aisle next to him. When they stood to sing or pray, his mother had to help hold him up. At one point during the service, the music team played the upbeat song "Amazing" by Matt Redman that repeats the words, "That's what's so amazing about your grace." The boy must have felt the vibrations from the deep bass sound with the drums and the saxophone because, all of a sudden, he wanted to stand up. He showed no concern that no one else was standing at this point, and neither did his mom. She stood and helped him stand up in the pew. Then, he took his little hand and pulled her chin toward him so he could read the words from her lips that she was singing. When he recognized the words "that's what's so amazing about your grace," he got very excited, and started clapping, and laughing, and jumping up and down. You've never seen such joy.

As the song ended and the congregation segued into the traditional version of "Amazing Grace," I doubled over in my lap and bawled—we're talking belly-shaking sobs. I prayed, "God, that's the joy I want back—just an unbridled passion for you and your grace!" And, in my spirit, I felt God answer my prayer from that morning, "Kim, if I can use this little boy—who is deaf and unable even to stand on his own—to spread joy, how dare you think I can't still use you?"

When Paul wrote that we should be joyful always, he wasn't referring to the everyday happiness that comes from the world, but being penetrated by the spiritual joy that comes from knowing that Christ died for us and he's coming back for us.

After all, when Kim prayed, "Just show me you love me" because "that's all that seemed to matter at the time," it's because that is all that really matters! Though we may be sad and hurting, we can rejoice always because we have a Savior who has rescued us from eternal death and who lives forever to intercede for us.

How do we get the same kind of vibrant existence that little boy in the pew exhibited? How do we practice constant joy? It starts with simply resolving to choose it. Being joyful doesn't mean we don't experience pain and suffering, but it does mean we get to choose our reactions to our pain. We can

be bitter and angry, or we can use our pain and become more beautiful, sympathetic, and joyful in spite of (and maybe even because of) it.

Anne Frank, who certainly could have become bitter after hiding from the Nazis for two years in an attic, said, "Think of all the beauty that's still left in and around you and be happy." Paul wrote, "We are experiencing all kinds of trouble, but we aren't crushed. We are confused, but we aren't depressed. We are harassed, but we aren't abandoned. We are knocked down, but we aren't knocked out." He said that all his pain was so the message of grace could reach more and more people. Though we may have a personal history that is blotted by suffering, we can choose to see it as inked by God for His greater design.

One month before Kim's mom was diagnosed with terminal cancer, she included a small cross in Kim's Christmas stocking that was engraved with the words of Nehemiah the prophet: "The joy of the LORD is my strength." In the coming months, she would experience constant and severe pain, loss of mobility, the loss of almost all her freedoms, and the knowledge that she would soon be losing her very life. Yet everyone marveled at how she refused to be marked by cancer; instead, she was marked by joy. If we can't think of any other reason to be joyful today, we can know that we have a Savior who loves us and has stamped us for eternal life.

Pray Continually

Dr. Andrew Newberg and Mark Robert Waldman use neuroimaging to study the impact of prayer on the brain. They write that active and positive spiritual belief changes our brains for the better, and that intense prayer permanently changes the configuration of our brains such that it actually changes our values and our perception of reality. Our friend Sylva said she thinks this is why prayer exists. "He already *knows.* But we tell stories differently, we think about situations with a different perspective, when we're telling them to God."

Twenty centuries before the scientific discovery of the positive impact of prayer on our brains, Paul wrote, "Don't be anxious about anything; rather bring up all of your requests to God in your prayers and petitions, along with giving thanks. Then the peace of God that exceeds all understanding will keep your hearts and minds safe in Christ Jesus."

Mark Batterson gives us a technical explanation of how Scripture reading and prayer work together. In his book *In a Pit with a Lion on a Snowy Day*, he says, "When we read Scripture, we are recruiting new nerve cells and rewiring neuronal connections. In a sense, we are downloading a new operating system that reconfigures the mind. We stop thinking human thoughts and start thinking God thoughts."

Batterson also talks about a cluster of nerve cells at the base of our brains called the reticular activating system (RAS). As we go about a typical day, our brains receive countless messages—

sights, sounds, and smells. We'd go crazy if we actually had to process all of those details, so the RAS stores the information in "files" so that we can recall them when we need to at a later time. That's how prayer works. Like tattoos that remind the imprinted of his or her story, Paul wrote that by constant prayer, we stay alert and keep praying for all believers. We also start to see opportunities to be involved in the solution.

We may not really understand how it all works, but we could share countless stories of how God has responded to our prayers. Once, during a particularly distressful time, Kim cried out loud to God, *"What is my purpose?"* In the next two weeks, she had three calls asking her to be a part of three different areas of ministry to young women. Another time, at 4:30 in the morning, too anxious to sleep because of some problem or other, she got a text from a friend in another city at that exact time: "Couldn't sleep. You're on my mind. Praying for you."

Janet once woke up in the middle of the night with a strong urge to pray for a former client whom she hadn't seen in years. Later, she ran into the woman and relayed the story to her. The woman smiled and told her, "It was at that time that I was seriously contemplating suicide."

One evening during a prayer group, five people we were praying for tried to contact us during that hour of prayer. The house phone rang, Janet's cell phone rang, Kim received a couple of text messages, and someone else sent an e-mail.

We love those moments. It is as if God says, "Now that you've prayed, I'm going to give you an opportunity to be involved in and witness the answer." God loves to do that for us. He loves to show us that His eyes are on us and His ears are open to our prayers. Telling each other how God has answered our prayers is encouraging. It's a way of picking up the speed of the fill for a friend who may have become numb to the Artist's work.

Give Thanks in All Circumstances

Our friend Joanne had been taking care of her mother-in-law for a couple of months. Margaret ("Ma," to those of us who loved her) was a petite, very gracious and sweet Sicilian with a quick sense of humor. But she had a lot of health issues, including diabetes and heart problems. Joanne was continuously monitoring Ma's heart rate, blood pressure, and insulin levels. One morning, Ma had to be taken to the hospital because she had woken up with one of her eyes completely crossed. They were concerned that it may have been caused by a stroke.

When Joanne relayed the story, Kim, displaying her usual lack of tact, blurted out: "Oh my gosh! Has it affected her vision?!" Let's see—*her eye is crossed! Of course* it affected her vision! But if Joanne thought Kim's comment insensitive, she didn't let on. Without skipping a beat, she responded, "Well, the good news is—that's her blind eye . . . ," and went right on talking.

Kim couldn't help herself. She started laughing. Joanne asked what was so funny, and after finally catching her breath, Kim said, "I'm sorry. I know I have a sick sense of humor, and this is terrible,

but imagine—'Ma woke up this morning with a crossed eye, but the good news is . . . that's her blind eye.' Exactly *how* bad do things have to be for your *blind* eye to be considered good news?"

After their laughter had died down, Joanne said, "Well, you can choose to see the glass half empty, or you can choose to see it half full. Or, in this case, you can be glad to see it at all!" Joanne is the ultimate example of one who gives thanks in all circumstances. To Joanne, there is *always* an upside.

Here are some of our thoughts on why God commands us to give thanks in all circumstances:

Being thankful teaches us to be optimistic. By looking at our blessings and not our deficits, we learn to think in terms of possibilities; not limitations.

Being thankful decreases our anxiety. Remember what Paul wrote to the Philippians? "Don't be anxious about anything; rather bring up all of your requests to God in your prayers and petitions, along with giving thanks. Then the peace of God that exceeds all understanding will keep your hearts and minds safe in Christ Jesus." Prayer was the first component and thanksgiving the second in the antidote to anxiety. Being thankful exhibits a trust in God's control over our lives.

Being thankful improves our relationships. We learn to appreciate the people in our lives, even with our challenges. When we pray for them, it changes our hearts toward them and we begin to look for ways to bless them.

Being thankful helps us see ourselves in the right light. We recognize our uniqueness in God. We appreciate how God has been working in us individually, which helps prevent comparisons, unhealthy competition, and jealousy. Comparing ourselves to others is destructive. God intends for you to be the best you and has equipped you with all you need to accomplish that.

Being thankful blesses those around us. We know a woman who has taught art for more than twenty years. When asked if any particular students stood out in her memory, she said, "Well, there was this one girl. . . . She would leave my class every day and say, 'Thank you, Mrs. A., for teaching us.' In all my years of teaching, no other student thanked me like that. You don't forget a student like that."

An attitude of gratitude benefits us physically, emotionally, spiritually, and relationally. So, how do we cultivate a thankful heart? For starters, begin a gratitude journal. Every single day, write something in it. Write down everything you're thankful for—material possessions, the people in your life, the talents God's gifted you with, your health, your freedom. Write down everything you can think of that you're thankful for and be as specific as possible. Even if you faced a challenge today, write down what you learned from the experience.

In *Walden*, Henry David Thoreau said, "To affect the quality of the day, that is the highest of the arts." To do just that, according to Norman Vincent Peale, Thoreau practiced a "good news technique." Every morning before his feet hit the floor, he would recite in his mind all the good news he could think of, Peale said,

"that he had a healthy body, that his mind was alert, that his work was interesting, that the future looked bright, and a lot of people trusted him."

And little things count. Audrey, a third grader, made her own gratitude journal, complete with cover art depicting some things she was thankful for. What was she thankful for? "Dear God, thank you for the shopping malls. Without them, we would have to drive from place to place." And, "Dear God, thank you for school. Even though we can catch germs there, we can still learn some pretty good stuff." The apostle Paul wrote that we should always give thanks to God the Father for everything!

At other times, it's hard to find anything to be thankful for, but the kids in a place called "The Hole" taught us to keep digging. When Kim traveled with a group of high school students on a mission trip to the Dominican Republic, they went to the poorest of the poor—a neighborhood dubbed "The Hole" by locals. The Hole is a landfill—the city trash heap. People can live there for free, as long as they're willing to live in squalor.

The Hole is run by a drug lord, prostitution is rampant, and girls who live there are typically pregnant by the time they're thirteen. Children run barefoot through pig feces. It would be easy in The Hole to give in to despair, yet there is a bright light there. A pastor has moved in and opened a feeding center, where the children are guaranteed to receive one hot meal a day, mostly white rice and a little piece of chicken.

On the day that Kim and the students visited to help serve lunch, countless kids—toddlers to teenagers—were filing into the small room and finding seats at the foldout tables. Before they were served, they bowed their heads and repeated after the pastor as he prayed: *"Gracias Señor, por nuestra comida."* (Thank you, Lord, for this food.) *"Gracias Señor, por las manos que la han hecho."* (Thank you, Lord, for the hands that made it.) *"Gracias Señor, por su Hijo, quien murió por nosotros."* (Thank you, Lord, for your Son who died for us.) And the thanks seemed to go on and on. Kim was so struck by their thankfulness—and by her own lack of thankfulness despite greater material abundance. Think you've got nothing to be thankful for? Kick it into third.

The Rewards Are SO Worth It

Janet recently reconnected with Barry, a kid she used to babysit for. He caught her up on what had happened in his life in the forty-some years since she'd last seen him. In his twenties, he started using drugs and suffered the consequences—financial problems, marital problems, legal problems, homelessness, you name it. Once, when he was stoned, he traded a bag of dope for a tattoo. While he sat in the kitchen, the scratcher tatooed a symbol resembling the cover of heavy metal band Godsmack's album *IV* on the inside of his wrist.

To Barry, the symbol signified power, making him feel as if he had taken back some of the control of his life. He'd soon discover just how out of control he was.

One night, after using cocaine most of the day, Barry ended up naked on the floor, his body bloodied from violently writhing on the carpet. Ironically, the iTunes review of the album from which Barry modeled his tattoo said it employs Godsmack's "usual themes of loneliness, betrayal, and the overuse of the word 'bleeding.'" Barry's wife got the minister on the phone, and Barry cried out to God to deliver him. After three and a half hours, he finally experienced what he describes as a supernatural release and indescribable peace.

Barry's long battle was over; he felt like a new man. But there on his arm was a constant reminder of the struggles and the shame of his past. He wanted the tattoo off, along with his memories. He underwent two laser removal treatments, which were very painful and required a month of healing between treatments. He was told it could take many more treatments to completely remove the symbol, so Barry decided to let go of the idea of getting rid of it.

He decided instead to think about it in a new way. A tattoo that once reminded him of a pain-filled life of guilt and shame is now a source of strength—an inked testament to what a loving, forgiving God did for him in his brokenness. Joyful, thankful, prayerful—that is the kind of new man Barry is. Joyful because God saved his life, thankful for God's forgiveness and redemption, and prayerful in all circumstances, as he knows that God is Lord of all and in all.

Kicking your thought life into third isn't easy. It's tough to resolve to be different in this world where it seems more in vogue to be marked with the morose, self-centered, and cynical. But the way of the trifecta is so worth it. Your Artist obviously thinks you can handle it. God's hand is on the dial, ready to kick it up, just waiting for you to give Him the nod. So set your jaw, fix your eyes on God, and aim to rejoice always, pray continually, and give thanks in every situation. As you do, you'll be surprised by the design that emerges.

Engrave It!

"What are you thankful for?" Janet posed this question to seminar participants for years and was touched by their responses. Inevitably, the top answers were not about material things but involved faith, family, friends, and freedom. What things are at the top of your list? Start now keeping a praise and gratitude journal. End each day by listing your blessings. (Even the little things count!)

Psalm 118:24 says, "This is the day the LORD has made; we will rejoice and be glad in it." Think about a time when you were truly happy. Write about it. What was it that made it special—the people with you? Lots of laughter? Surprise? Nature? Simple things? Practice giving thanks for these simple gifts!

The Look: Seeing Your Tat for the First Time

By the grace of God I am what I am, and his grace to me was not without effect.

—1 Corinthians 15:10 (NIV)

I am a canvas of my experiences, my story is etched in lines and shading, and you can read it on my arms, my legs, my shoulders, and my stomach. But like everybody else, I was born naked and screaming, waiting for my life to write itself on my skin.

—*Kat Von D,* High Voltage Tattoo

Tattoo artist Julie Rose posted on her blog the story of a retired military man who came to her for a tattoo on his forearm—an eagle with a tattered flag waving in the background. After four hours, the client paid her and Rose was satisfied with a job well done. About twenty-four hours later, after the client had removed the bandages, he called sounding very upset: "Can you cover up red with white ink?" After explaining that no she couldn't, it would just turn out pink, Rose said the customer then began to half cry, half yell at her.

Even though she'd checked the art and asked the client to double-check it, the stripes on the flag weren't in the correct order. The stripe just underneath the stars should be white. His was red. He started talking about laser removal. Hoping he wouldn't go to that length, Rose offered to refund his money and told him that if he didn't point it out to people, they wouldn't notice. The client didn't believe her and was especially concerned about the scrutinizing eyes of his military friends.

Later Rose discovered that about half of the flash art that exists of the American flag is incorrect. She started asking military clients to take a look at hers and said that not one of them ever identified the incorrect flags. She wrote, "I think back on that man, who sounded like he was going to cry, and hope that he hasn't spent all these years pointing out the mistake to others. It was a good tattoo and people just don't look that closely."

In tattoo lingo, "The Look" is the telltale smile and look of admiration when a person sees his new tattoo for the first time. Even though the fresh tattoo is red and raw and gooey from the ointment, the customer sees its potential, not what it currently is. Unfortunately, like Julie Rose's client, rather than a look of admiration, we often give ourselves looks of regret and self-condemnation. We're hard on each other. And even if no one else notices, we're our own worst critics, exaggerating our shortcomings and focusing on our flaws.

For women, that kind of toxic ink is perhaps worst in the area of body image. In an effort to rub out that ink, the Lifetime TV show *How to Look Good Naked* tried to get women to recognize their assets and to see themselves the way others see them. The show used tactics like displaying a big poster of the guest in her undies on a tall city building and asking passersby what they think of the model. The woman would watch off-camera, in tears as she would hear people compliment her. If that didn't work to change her mind, the host would take her to a wall of belts of different sizes, all fastened and hanging in circles, and would ask the woman to select her belt size. Inevitably, she would pick a belt much too big for her waist.

The Look can be blurred even more when we compare ourselves to others. In yet another tactic of the show, a row of ten women lined up in order of size, smallest to biggest. The participant was then asked to go stand between the two women where she thought she fit in order of size. Time after time, the participant consistently would put herself in a position on the line that was about four places bigger than where she should have been. Her perception of herself was all wrong; her mind's eye had added about six inches to her hips!

The apostle Peter got into trouble when trying to compare himself to another. As he was walking along the shores of the Sea of Galilee with Jesus, Jesus asked him three times whether he loved him. After the third time, exasperated, Peter answered, "Lord, you know all things; you know that I love you." Then Jesus said, "Follow me!" But Peter took his eyes off his Artist and looked behind him to see the apostle John following some distance behind. "What about him?" he asked. And Jesus said to Peter what he says to us: "What is that to you? You must follow me." In other words, don't worry what anyone else is inked with; you choose me, and I'll emblazon you with your own unique mark.

The apostle Paul wrote that God in his grace has marked us all with different designs. Our unique marks are to be appreciated in each other and used for the common good. When we focus on our Artist and on what we have been marked for, we don't have time to compare ourselves to others. In the same way that it's not a good idea to get a gang-related tattoo if you're not a member, your Artist says, "Don't try to take on someone else's marks. Just be who I made you to be." Because when you do, and when everyone else does, a beautiful design emerges.

The Look can also be distorted by others' opinions of us. Sara, a high school senior, cried as she told us about an argument she'd recently had with her dad. She had walked into the house wearing something he wasn't comfortable seeing his tall, beautiful, athletically built daughter wearing. Never mind whether the outfit really was inappropriate or whether this dad was all of a sudden freaking out that his baby girl was about to go off to college and he's about to lose all control. What's relevant is that the argument became rather heated, and in the course of it, this Christian father ended up calling his daughter a slut.

His comment had the potential to permeate some serious poison ink. But as Sara continued to cry, a very powerful thing happened. Someone in the group cut through her sobs and simply asked, "What's the truth?"

As Sara quieted and looked up, wiping her nose, she continued:

> The truth is you are a beautiful, strong, smart child of God. You may have made a poor decision, but you are not a slut. And, the truth is, your dad is a godly man who is just scared of losing his daughter and knows how boys think and is wondering at the eleventh hour, "Have I done it right? Did I teach her everything she needs to know before she goes off on her own?" Your dad was wrong to say that. You are at a critical time when you need his hugs and his affirmation, and his behavior did not meet your expectations. But here is an opportunity for you—you can go negative and pull away from your dad, or you can choose to show him some grace and grow toward your dad.

Mastering the Voices

So what *is* the truth? John Forbes Nash Jr. is a brilliant mathematician who has been a huge influence on gaming, market economics, military applications, computing, and artificial intelligence. In 1994, he won the Nobel Memorial Prize for Economic Sciences. His list of accolades goes on, yet he has had a terrible time discerning the truth. A large part of his life has been marked by auditory hallucinations and delusions—including the belief that an organization full of characters wearing red ties was chasing him.

Near the end of the movie *A Beautiful Mind*, based on Nash's life, we see Nash (played by Russell Crowe) starting to overcome the struggle with discerning the truth when he tearfully says good-bye to his hallucinated "friends" and tells them he won't be speaking with them any longer. Despite what his eyes and ears may have told him, he had learned the truth. Ultimately, we hear a voice-over from Nash's character: "We all hear voices. We just have to decide which ones we are going to listen to."

Whatever the source, we all have to learn to master the voices. In a highly acclaimed book on self-esteem, Dr. Matthew McKay and Patrick Fanning say that our life circumstances only indirectly account for our self-esteem (or the lack thereof). However, they say there's one factor that determines self-esteem 100 percent of the time: our thoughts.

Kat von D, inked-from-head-to-toe owner of High Voltage Tattoo and famous for her work on the TV show *LA Ink*, wrote:

"When you look at my body, you can see my memories." And, in fact, how we choose to think about ourselves and our experiences, what we allow to be inked on ourselves, is so important that it can inspire us to live out our calling or it can cause unspeakable damage. We need to learn to master the voices.

But how do we even go about making that sort of change in thinking? It starts with spending time in the chair, examining the marks that have been made, and allowing the Artist to remove the faulty marks and engrave new ones in their place. We call it Reveal, Rub Out, and Reink.

Reveal

Think of Sara, when her dad called her a slut. Unless thoughts like those are challenged, what happens is the brain stores that memory so that every time that memory is triggered (when she's getting ready for a date, for example), Sara will go through the original feelings of shame, hurt, and anger all over again. The brain taps into that deeply ingrained toxic ink and the feelings associated with it appear all over again.

Unless Sara learns to reveal that ink for the toxin it is, she'll struggle with it for the rest of her life. Even if she thinks she's doing a good job of suppressing those contaminated thoughts, Dr. Caroline Leaf said they will eventually come out in attitudes like perfectionism, a desire for control, self-doubt, cynicism, criticism, promiscuity, and a tendency to overreact—all poison ink

that, unless rubbed out, can permeate her heart, affect her health, and rob her of peace and joy. Sure, she can try to hide the permeated ink, but a cancerous design will be the result.

If it's better to expose the bad ink for what it is, how do you first recognize it? According to Albert Ellis, psychologist and father of the cognitive behavior therapies, toxic ink comes from one of three beliefs: I must do well. You must treat me well. The world must be easy.

These may sound harmless, but Leaf said that if we look at these kinds of statements and the feelings they generate in us, we'll recognize how they don't serve us well. "In real life," she said, "no one does well all the time, everyone is mistreated sometimes, and life is not always easy or fair. Demanding unrealistic performance from yourself and others puts your mind and body in stress mode and thus has a negative effect on your health."

So we have to listen to how we talk to ourselves. Are we critical? Do we use absolute thinking (words like *always*, *never*, and *should*)? Do we hear ourselves indicating that we have to be perfect or else we're a total failure, with no in-between? Do we use negative talk about others or the world around us?

Poison ink is the ink that blames us for things that go wrong, compares us to others, and decides that we don't quite make the mark. It's the ink that draws lines of perfection and draws a big red X when we don't meet it. It creates a portfolio of our shortcomings and the injustices done to us, rather than of our strengths and the blessings showered upon us.

So we have to start by revealing the toxic ink. It can be hard to identify, but journaling helps, especially when we're having strong emotions about something. If we write down what we're feeling, we're able to better zero in on the toxic ink. Once it's revealed, we can begin to rub it out and ink healthier remarks on our hearts and minds.

Rub Out and Reink

When Julie decided to go back to college at thirty-something, she was filled with the ink of doubt and insecurity. She questioned whether the other students would think she was too old, whether she would fit in, and if her mind was as sharp as it used to be. On the first day of her psychology class, she found a seat in the large lecture hall. After the girl sitting next to her got up and moved, Julie spent a good amount of that class retracing the lines of some old ink. Ink that assumed the girl must have moved because she didn't want to sit next to an older person. Ink that in shorthand read: Old. Stupid. Don't belong.

Luckily, the girl later approached Julie to tell her she had moved because a structural column was blocking her view of the professor. If she hadn't, Julie would have continued to retrace toxic ink that would deface her sense of self. Paul wrote that we have God-powered tools to rub out the toxic ink—prayer and scripture. He said it's with those tools that we capture every thought to make it line up with Christ. If it doesn't line up with what you know to be your Artist's true design for you, rub it out.

Through Scripture and prayer, God will show us truth and expose the toxic lies that have been inked on our minds. We can also learn to be overt in clarifying our assumptions.

Kim once got into a lot of hot water at work over a misunderstanding. The human resources manager called her on her morning commute and said they needed to have a meeting as soon as Kim got into the office. When Kim arrived, her own boss as well as another manager was in the room. At the company picnic the day before, a very pregnant coworker thought she overheard Kim calling her chubby.

Everyone in that office knew that name-calling, most of all directed at pregnant women, wasn't characteristic of Kim. Still, the lady was sure she knew what she had heard and she was very upset. What's more, she was an integral part of Kim's client's team, and she was threatening that she could no longer work on the same team.

After a full day of racking her brain, it dawned on Kim that she had been talking to another coworker at the picnic about how much she loved Ben and Jerry's Chubby Hubby flavor of ice cream. The pregnant coworker's last name sounded very similar to "Hubby." It would have been akin to a man nicknamed "Bubby" overhearing "Chubby Bubby." Had the woman only immediately and directly asked Kim at the picnic, it would have prevented the wrong ink from settling in for a full twenty-four hours.

We don't have to spend years rubbing out the lies and reinking the truth. Spending enough time to dig and find the sources and experiences that underlie some of our toxic ink can be a beneficial start. Once these beliefs are examined in light of truth, the toxic ink can be rubbed out and our Artist's design can be reinked.

Somewhere Between Broken and Bold

As one of the nation's top weight lifters, Giff Reed was marked by a dream to compete in the Olympics. He trained every day for six months at the Olympic Training Center in Colorado Springs in hopes of making the 2004 team. That year, just three men made the US Olympic weight-lifting team. Giff was ranked ninth in the nation—just six spots away from achieving his dream of being in the Olympics. What followed was an identity crisis. When he didn't make it, he said he came to a stark realization of his own insecurities and brokenness. He asked himself: "Who *am* I without weightlifting? What is my identity?"

Rather than wallow in ink that could have discolored his identity for the rest of his life, Giff got in the chair and spent some time with his Artist. With Scripture and prayer, he felt God impressing upon him the scriptural truth that the kind of offering God desires is a broken spirit and a contrite heart. Giff said he humbly realized that, top athlete or not, he was *broken*, and he needed to keep the fact that he was just like any other man in need of redemption in the forefront.

On the other hand, while in the chair seeking a new identity, he said he also felt that God was calling him to be *bold*. Pointing to the passage in Hebrews that says that we are able to approach

God's throne with confidence in order to receive mercy and grace when we need it, Giff realized, "Yes, I'm broken and in need of redemption, but God expects me to approach him boldly. We don't *crawl* to the throne of grace."

He said he feels like he needs both—that acting too broken can lead to being overly contrite with a "woe is me" outlook (and not where God intends for us to stay), but that too much of the other—boldness—can lead to arrogance. He admitted, "I'm really broken, but that doesn't mean I wallow in it." To always remind him that he lives in the tension between brokenness and boldness, on one upper arm he has tattooed in Hebrew the psalmist's phrase "a broken and contrite heart." On the other, in Greek, the word *boldness*. Giff said he feels like he will forever be living in the balance between the two and that he never wants to forget the power that's available to him. He may not have made the Olympics, but Giff knows firsthand the power that is made perfect in weakness.

Giff understands that in order to rub out the toxic ink and be reinked with the truth, we have to understand who we are as we sit in that chair in front of our Artist. What is the bare truth of who we are in God? It's somewhere between broken and bold.

When the apostle Paul despaired over his own "thorn in the flesh," he called out to his Artist three times to remove it. Scholars have long debated exactly what this thorn was, and we don't know for sure. What we do know is that the Greek for "thorn" in this passage is *skólops*, and it's defined as anything with a sharp point or, figuratively, an instrument producing pain. Whatever it was and for whatever reason, the Artist didn't remove it. Instead, He said to Paul, "My grace is sufficient for you, for my power is made perfect in weakness."

Paul knew about brokenness. But he also knew about boldness. After all, he's the one who said that because of our faith in Christ, we have bold and confident access to God. The one and true God of the universe loves us. What would it mean if we went about our day actually believing *that* ink? What if we went about treating others as if it were also true about them? What kind of designs would emerge?

From Old Glory to Ever-Increasing Glory

When Julie Rose's client took his first look at "Old Glory" on his forearm, he didn't experience that "telltale smile and look of admiration." He focused on the flaws to the point of despair. If he could look past his flawed tattoo to his true mark—the stamp of God's power reflected in a courageous man—well, he'd be in good company.

Think of Moses. After spending forty days and nights alone with God on Mount Sinai, Moses had The Look. When he returned to camp, the book of Exodus describes that his face was so radiant from having been with God that he had to put a veil over his face so the people could look at him.

The lesson is profound: we must spend a sufficient amount of time in the Artist's chair before we can reveal a radiant design to the world. Just as the apostle John wrote, "We love because God first loved us," we can't fully make our mark on the world until we've spent time in the chair, allowing Him to make His mark on us. There was one who was pierced for our rebellion, and it's by *his* stripes (his whippings) that we are healed.

Rose's client should be proud of his brave defense of Old Glory, but he should know that Paul wrote of a New Glory: "In fact, what was glorious isn't glorious now, because of the glory that is brighter. If the glory that fades away was glorious, how much more glorious is the one that lasts!"

There's a different kind of freedom for us, not one gained by military strength, but the one Paul described when he said, "Where the Lord's Spirit is, there is freedom. All of us are looking with unveiled faces at the glory of the Lord as if we were looking in a mirror. We're being transformed into that same image from one degree of glory to the next degree of glory."

We all have a glory that comes from the Lord. Christ bought your freedom on the cross. *You* are his glory.

Engrave It!

Reveal, Rub Out, and Reink.

1. Make a list of the poison ink that is prominent in your thinking because of things people have said about you, or some messages you've said to yourself. You may even need to keep a small notebook with you and, when you catch yourself using any toxic ink in your self-talk, write it down. Include words that make you feel inferior (for example, *loser/fat/stupid*), words that are defeating (*I can't/I'll never*) and words that are perfectionist (*I should have/I shouldn't have*).
2. Once you've rubbed out the poison ink, you're left with some pretty deep gashes—*unless* you fill up those gashes with truths about yourself. Cross out the poison ink and next to it add a scriptural truth (a word, phrase, or complete verse) that will reink the truth. Make a list of truths for every toxic thought you struggle with. Tape them to your bathroom mirror, the dashboard of your car, your school locker, your computer at work. With time, you'll be revealing, rubbing out, and reinking the toxic ink like a true apprentice to the Master Artist.
3. List three people in your life who support a positive, God-affirming imprint on you. Commit to spending regular time with those people. And be sure to tell them what their presence in your life means to you.

Chapter 7

Works in Progress: Meeting Others in the Tattoo Shop

There's no distinction.

All have sinned and fall short of God's glory.

—Romans 3:22b-23

Tattoo. What a loaded word it is, rife with associations to goons, goofs, bikers, tribal warriors, carnival artists, drunken sailors and floozies.

—Jon Anderson

At first glance, we might imagine heavily tattooed Eric to be in the middle of an identity crisis. He has some older, rudimentary-looking designs: a pair of dice (a 3 and a 4—lucky number 7), a cross, the word *Dad*, a skull. There are others that appear to have been done by a better artist: Asian masks, a wizard, and a beautiful koi that seems to turn into a dragon. On his left arm are side-by-side smiling faces of a man and a woman. On his back is the most surprising of all—a beautiful, realistic portrait of the face of Jesus. And not the serene Anglo-Saxon face of Jesus. This is the Jesus in anguish, the suffering Jesus with the crown of thorns.

A little bit of luck, a little bit of magic, and a little bit of Jesus thrown in for good measure.

But Eric isn't just paying tribute to many different themes. Rather, the tattoos on the outer man tell a progressive, but no less miraculous, story of the changes branded on his inner man.

Known and watched by the police from his teen years, Eric and his friends wanted to be like the heroes they read about in their biker magazines. The articles, frequently written by prison inmates, glorified the criminal lifestyle. While Eric went to church to appease his mom, he was secretly into drugs and alcohol. By age fifteen, he had picked on his skin the dice, cross, and *Dad*

tattoos himself, and later let a friend use a homemade tattoo machine to fashion some improvements to his original artwork.

By the time Eric was seventeen, he was stealing. Once, while transporting stolen guns, another car began tailgating him and his buddies. Afraid it might be an undercover cop, Eric's accomplice fired a gun at the car and blasted out the windshield. Eventually, they were apprehended and taken to the county jail. Eric wanted to be seen as a tough guy, a man, so he lied to the police and told them he was twenty years old. They believed him and he was put in jail with the adult male inmates until he was sentenced ten months later.

Originally sentenced to four years, his incarceration was lengthened by a year for contempt when he refused to testify against his friends. Eric did his time and was released, only to be arrested again a month later on a parole violation for drinking and attempted theft. Finding himself back in prison for another two and a half years, he told himself this was the last time.

Once finally on the outside again, though, his life didn't change overnight. He would go through a divorce and recovery from drug and alcohol abuse. His outer appearance reflects his inner confusion at that time—the skull, the masks, the wizard. The koi morphing into a dragon comes from a Chinese legend that if a koi can make it upstream and out of the water, it turns into a dragon, representing strength and power.

Then Eric fell in love—with the woman on his bicep—and married her. But as they began their lives together, something kept nagging at him. There was still a hole that couldn't be filled.

The luck, the magic, the mask-wearing, the struggling to swim upstream, even the love of another person was not enough to satisfy. Desperate to find what would satisfy, he found himself back in church and soon after encountered the only true source of strength and power. Eric committed his life to Christ, choosing to no longer be conformed to the pattern of this world but to allow Christ to transform him by renewing his mind.

Wanting a new tattoo to signify his inner change, he finally found just the right design—in a picture puzzle in a vending machine in a Goodwill store. Eric began buying the pieces, spending one quarter at a time. After repeatedly getting the same pieces, Eric went to the store manager and asked if she could open the machine so he could get all the different pieces to the puzzle. She couldn't, but Eric was undeterred. He got a fist full of quarters and kept at it until he had the whole thing.

That puzzle served as the art for his latest tattoo. Taking twenty-five hours to complete, the tortured Christ is the largest and most impressive. Smudged with a bad-boy image by age seven-

teen, little did Eric know that his Artist would perfectly fit together those jagged pieces of his life to create a masterpiece that glorifies God.

Not only does his outer ink tell the world that he is a new man in Christ, but his heart has also been permanently marked by his time in the chair. This former bad-boy biker now often rises before dawn to join the Redeemed Riders chapter of the Christian Motorcycle Association, serving prisons throughout the state of Indiana. Their motto? "Changing one heart at a time."

What Counts Is a New Creation

Walk into any tattoo shop today and you may meet someone with the full-body coverage of a carnival artist, a biker with tattooed sleeves, a stay-at-home mother with a small butterfly on her foot, or a teenager with music lyrics inked on his back.

And yet there are still those with a strong aversion to ink or at least some prejudices toward certain types of ink. The apostle Peter once had an aversion to other clients of the same Artist too. He was considered one of the three in Jesus' inner circle of friends, but Peter would not have even dreamed of sitting down to a meal with anyone who was not a Jew.

Until he did. Have a dream, that is. In his dream, a sheet came down from heaven with all kinds of so-called "unclean" animals on it—animals that he, as a Jew, had been forbidden to eat. In his dream, a voice said, "Never consider unclean what God has made

pure." The very next day, meeting with a large group of Gentiles, Peter said, "I really am learning that God doesn't show partiality to one group of people over another."

Let's be honest. We say we believe we're all made in God's image, but with the same tongue we use to praise God, we curse those who are made in God's likeness. We encounter the other works in progress in the tattoo shop and we shun, judge, gossip about, and condemn them.

But couldn't we take Jon Anderson's quotation from the beginning of this chapter and substitute "Christian" for "tattoo"? *Christian. What a loaded word it is, rife with associations to addicts, adulterers, idolaters, and all kinds of sinners.* Does that ink rub you the wrong way? What about Saul, the persecutor of Christians? What about the liar, murderer, and adulterer King David? What about the prostitute Rahab? Talk about your goons, goofs, and floozies. Yet Saul, once a persecutor of Christians, became Christianity's most impactful missionary to the world; God called King David a man after his own heart; and Rahab helped the Israelite spies and was counted in the genealogy of Jesus. When we take a close look at history and at our own hearts, we can be glad that God has said, "Humans see only what is visible to the eyes, but the LORD sees into the heart."

Since we don't see into the heart, we often avoid, at best, and slander, at worst, those who are different. We conveniently forget that we've all sinned and fall short of God's glory. But what if we took to heart our Artist's wish, expressed in his prayer before he was arrested a prayer that was not only for believers of that time, but for us as well?

> I pray they will be one, Father, just as you are in me and I am in you. I pray that they also will be in us, so that the world will believe that you sent me. I've given them the glory that you gave me so that they can be one just as we are one. I'm in them and you are in me so that they will be made perfectly one. Then the world will know that you sent me and that you have loved them just as you loved me.

Complete unity. What would that even look like?

One of the best displays of unity we've seen expressed through tattoo comes from Amsterdam. In 2004, to protest Queen Beatrix's order that the national anthem of the Netherlands, "Wilhelmus," be played only in the presence of the royal family, famous tattooist Henk Schiffmacher selected a cross section of thirty-three Dutch citizens and tattooed each of them with one word from the first verse of the anthem. These "Knights of the 'Wilhelmus'" varied in age from twenty-five to seventy and came from all walks of life. According to a news service, "After applying the tattoo, Schiffmacher patted the wound of each word dry with blotting paper. In this way, he created the entire verse in blood, to be presented to the Queen." Blood that was shed to champion unity.

Our unique experiences mark us individually, yet when we choose to be inked by Christ, we become unified in one body. *May they be brought to complete unity to let the world know that you sent me and have loved them even as you have loved me.*

Complete unity. How do we get there?

Polynesians have a rich history of tattooing bold, black symbols that display their personal history. So when anthropologist Tricia Allen wanted to do fieldwork in the Pacific, she felt that it would be easier to approach and understand this population as a tattooist rather than as an academic. She became a tattoo artist specializing in Polynesian tattoos. In a similar way, Jesus didn't consider his deity something to exploit but emptied himself by becoming one of us.

Paul wrote that if we get any encouragement from Christ's love, then we should have the same love, and be united in spirit and purpose. In fact, he called love "the perfect bond of unity." And, he said the Artist creates us all differently *exactly so that* the body of Christ may be built up and so that we will all reach unity. Unity in Christ is not about everyone being the same. After all, Jesus' disciples were a mix of fishermen, tax collectors, doctors, businesspeople, religious leaders, soldiers, and homemakers. We're created uniquely so that when we're united in love, the body of Christ is more diverse, stronger, more beautiful.

When Jesus said that the greatest commandment is to love God with all your heart and with all your soul and with all your strength and with all your mind and that the second greatest is to love your neighbor, the lawyer he was talking to decided to split hairs: "But what do you mean by 'neighbor'?" The attorneys get involved and we have to add an addendum that describes what we mean by "neighbor."

That addendum is found in the parable of the good Samaritan. A Jewish man had been attacked by bandits and left for dead on the side of the road. His own people—a Jewish priest and a Levite (who was of the tribe set apart for special service in the temple)—both passed him by without helping. Then a Samaritan came along. If the victim's only countrymen passed him by, then surely a Samaritan, an enemy to the Jews, would not do better. But the parable reads almost like a riddle: "So, a priest, a Levite, and a Samaritan pass a dying man on the road. Which one was his neighbor?" Then there's the punch line: "the detestable Samaritan!" Why? Because he's the one who showed mercy.

There's a sign that's often seen in tattoo shops: "The only difference between a tattooed person and a person who isn't tattooed is that a tattooed person doesn't care if you're tattooed or not." The Samaritan, then, at least spiritually speaking, had a tattoo. The Samaritan, marked as abhorrent to the Jews, did not care how the dying man was identified. He bandaged the man's wounds, cared for him, and moved toward unity. And Jesus said to the lawyer, "Go and do likewise."

Where to Start?

How can we take all these prejudices and fears and mistrusts of each other and move toward unity? Why not start the same way we develop any relationship—by showing interest in each other? "When you start to have visible tattoos, you will find that people treat you a little differently," said John Reardon. "People might stare at you more. Many people will talk to you about your tattoos and even try to touch you. It sounds freaky, but it's true. If you are polite about it, people will often be very polite back to you." The opening question doesn't have to be about tattoos. But what if we tried it? What if we broke out of our shells and approached someone who doesn't look like us, and said, "Tell me about your tattoo. Is there a story behind it?"

In this age of mass communication, amid a plague of "text loneliness" and one thousand–plus Facebook "friends," we guarantee that people are starving to know that you see them. After all, tattoos have been called one of the most democratic forms of expression.

Here's a riddle for you: What's four inches long, has been used by Billy Graham to win more than three million souls to Christ, and by Hitler to bring about the annihilation of six million Jews?

It's been likened to both a bit in a horse's mouth, able to move the animal anywhere we want it to go, and a rudder that is able to move an entire ship. With it we have the ability to both praise God and to curse our fellow humans. It's the tongue. And this dynamic tool has the power to convey love, encourage others, comfort the hurting, even save lives—or to criticize, condemn, complain, or utterly destroy lives.

The canvas of history oozes with the wounds pierced by a sharp tongue. Russ Blowers was preaching at a revival years ago at the Mars View Christian Church on the south side of

Indianapolis. Russ told an interesting story about the revival. There was a tremendous number of people there, and they were excited about the week they had in store for them. They had a pianist who was doing a beautiful job, and Russ went to talk with her about an invitation song. He met Agnes, who told him that she was the sister of John Dillinger, perhaps the greatest gangster of the 1930s. She explained how John had been a rebellious child and was always causing trouble. He came to church once and caused problems. He was loud, he was crude, and many were turned away from him. He came a second week and was acting in the same manner. This time the preacher told him that he would never amount to anything and for him to never come back to the church again. John never did come back to church again. He became the mobster. As Agnes and Russ finished their conversation, she looked at him and told him to preach salvation to everyone who was there—they needed to hear the truth. They deserved to know that God is a God of second chances.

John Dillinger's life might have been different had good ink been infused into his life—people affirming him, rather than giving him negative messages.

Instead, Dillinger performed like the students in Dr. Robert Rosenthal's famous Pygmalion experiment, who performed to their teachers' expectations—whether positive or negative.

In his study in the 1960s, Rosenthal told teachers that students in first through sixth grades were taking a test called the Harvard Test of Inflected Acquisition, which was supposed to indicate how quickly a student would grow academically. Teachers were then told which students scored in the top 20 percent. In reality, however, those names were picked at random. The results showed that the students whom teachers expected to be smarter actually did increase their real IQ scores significantly. It had nothing to do with how smart they actually were but, rather, how their teachers treated them based on preconceived notions.

It's like when Harry Potter pretended to slip some *Felix Felicis* ("Liquid Luck") potion into Ron's drink so that he'd play well in the quidditch game. It wasn't until the after-party, where Ron was being celebrated as the hero, when he discovered he performed well on his own abilities. Harry had just helped his confidence.

People rise or sink to our levels of expectation. Resilience research shows that if just one person takes a stand for another, regardless of circumstances, it can make a difference in the entire trajectory of that person's life. So consider carefully what we ink onto others. Make an effort to tell others what talents and positive qualities you see in them. Long before research supported it, Paul wrote, "Do not let any unwholesome talk come out of your mouths, but only what is helpful for building others up."

The apostle James wrote that the tongue is a world of evil at work within us. As one commentator points out:

> Who can measure the evils which arise from scandal, and slander, and profaneness, and perjury, and falsehood, and blasphemy, and obscenity, and the inculcation of error, by the tongue? Who can gauge the amount of broils, and contentions, and strifes, and wars, and suspicions, and enmities, and alienations among friends and neighbors, which it produces? Who

> can number the evils produced by the "honeyed" words of the seducer; or by the tongue of the eloquent in the maintenance of error, and the defense of wrong? If all men were dumb, what a portion of the crimes of the world would soon cease! If all men would speak only that which ought to be spoken, what a change would come over the face of human affairs!

Who can measure the loss? Who can gauge the damage?

Dr. Caroline Leaf described how our hearts communicate with our brains through nerve impulses, hormones, neurotransmitters, pressure waves, and (new evidence suggests) through electromagnetic field interactions. She said there's new scientific evidence "that points to feedback loops between the brain and the heart that check the accuracy and integrity of our thought life." Gives new meaning to Jesus' words that what goes out of the mouth comes from the heart, doesn't it? And what goes out of the mouth has the power to be a work of evil or a tool for unity.

Filler

To move toward unity, we have a responsibility not only for the marks we make on others but also for the ink we allow to settle into our own pores. Sometimes people don't meet our expectations. They let us down. Your roommate is late again on her half of the rent. Your dad breaks another promise to show up for your game. Your husband splurges on a big-ticket item without talking it over with you first. Your best friend deserts you in your darkest hour. People will disappoint us. And it can really mess with our heads.

It's like going in for a full upper-body tattoo and getting only sleeves—and the sleeves don't even match. Stretch out your arms, as far apart from each other as you can get them. Imagine that one sleeve is what you expected, but the other sleeve represents how the other person actually behaved. The two are completely disconnected. What do you do with all that blank space in the middle?

In Ina Saltz's photographic book of tattoos, there's a striking picture of the length of a young man's forearm. Centered at the inside of his elbow is a skull. Running from the skull's chin, from about two inches from his inner elbow to his wrist, his arm is almost completely filled with black ink. If you look at the photo closely, you will see that the black ink covers raised letters running down the length of his forearm: HATRED. The caption explains that he burned the letters into his arm when he was just sixteen, after his mother killed herself and left him alone. A few years later, he covered over the letters with black ink, with the exception of one word that is dropped out of the sleeve in relief fashion. The one word that appears through the black ink? FORGIVEN.

When someone disappoints us and doesn't meet our expectations, we need some filler. Filler is a design that will connect the two sleeves so that they flow into each other and create a unified design. And that filler is forgiveness.

However much filler we decide to use in this space determines the future direction of our relationship with people. If we leave the space blank, we can let bitterness and disappointment settle in the space and the relationship will be forever damaged. If we forgive them and free ourselves from any claim their behavior had on us—on our emotions, energy, thought lives, and even our health—we get a chance to build the relationship.

Easier said than done, we know.

Three other photos in Saltz's book also relate to forgiveness. Interestingly, all of them are about harms caused by parents. One, written just below his inside elbow, is a message for the young man's father: "le acepto y perdono." (I accept and forgive you.) But the other two spell UNFORGIVEN down the length of their forearms ("a declaration to their fathers that they could never forgive them"). They permanently inked a reminder where they would be sure to see it every day for the rest of their lives. Their inability to forgive has kept them forever in bondage to the ones who have harmed them.

The Artist tells you to consider carefully what you'll do with the forgiveness filler, because there will be a time when you won't meet someone's expectations. Jesus says, "Don't judge, and you won't be judged. Don't condemn, and you won't be condemned. Forgive, and you will be forgiven. Give, and it will be given to you. A good portion—packed down, firmly shaken, and overflowing—will fall into your lap. The portion you give will determine the portion you receive in return."

A friend of ours saw the forgiveness filler inked in a dramatic way. Two leaders of rival gangs were attending the same alternative school that our friend founded. These gang members were used to fighting; in fact, they'd actually shot at each other. Our friend sat them both down and said, "Look. This is the last stop for both of you. Next stop is a juvenile detention center. Your only hope—if you care about your futures—is to find a way to get along." They ended up discovering that they both loved basketball, so they formed a community team that they co-led. Their team ended up winning the community tournament, and the local paper displayed a picture of them, arm in arm (you might even say with their sleeves connected), trophy held high.

However we do it, Jesus felt that inking this forgiveness filler was even more important than worship. He tells us that even if we're in the middle of offering worship and we remember a void that exists between us and someone else, we should stop right there and go find the person and fill the void. In essence, he says, "Don't come with love for me, and yet have anger or hatred in your heart for one of my children." Sure, it'll take guts to go to the other person and offer peace. But even if they don't accept it immediately, we can go back and worship with joy, knowing that we've done the thing that God requires of us.

The One-Percenters

In the 1950s, although the American Motorcycle Association claims that it was a misquote, the AMA allegedly issued a statement that 99 percent of bikers were law-abiding citizens. In retaliation, the Hells Angels and similar clubs decided they would be in the 1 percent. And in response, many bikers in those clubs were tattooed with "1%ER."

According to a study of more than one thousand young adults ages eighteen to thirty, 70 percent stop attending church for at least a year between the ages of eighteen and twenty-two. We expected many of the reasons cited in the top ten, such as college was keeping them too busy, or they had moved away from their home church and just hadn't got back into the swing of things. But the two reasons in the top ten that should give the church pause were: (1) "church members seemed judgmental or hypocritical"; and (2) "didn't feel connected to the people in my church."

Judgmental and unfriendly. In a religion whose leader says the second greatest commandment is to "love others as yourself," whose leader's last prayer was that his followers would have complete unity, whose leader commands his believers to show mercy and offer forgiveness, 70 percent of young people are leaving the church because its members are unfriendly and judgmental.

Just as we were putting the finishing touches on this book, our editor shared with us a news article out of Houston, Texas. Entering the Lenten season, Chris Seay, pastor of Ecclesia, asked for volunteers from his church to be tattooed with images from the crucifixion of Christ for an interactive art exhibit called Stations on Skin. Fifty church members answered the call and were tattooed with abstract designs of the stations of the cross.

Tattooist Scott Erickson chose Russian prison–style and Sailor Jerry–style tattoos as his design inspiration. His hope in doing so

was that the tattoos would invite more conversation and open doors to discuss Jesus, whereas traditional crosses and pictures of Jesus' face have become so ubiquitous that they may no longer do so.

"Like one from whom men hide their faces," the prophet Isaiah wrote, "he was despised, and we esteemed him not." Even though he took up our infirmities and carried our sorrows, "we considered him stricken by God, smitten by him, and afflicted." And while our own arms are still outstretched and we're looking down at that empty space, wondering what kind of filler needs to go there, consider that he once held that same position—only he was lifted high on a cross and was pierced in order to fill the gap for all of us goons, goofs, and floozies. And it is by his wounds we are healed.

Engrave It!

Try your own Pygmalion effect experiment. It's been said that everyone needs to hear three things: (1) "I love you"; (2) "I'm proud of you"; and (3) "You're good at [fill-in-the-blank]." Try saying these to someone (in your own words, and not necessarily all at once!) and see if they seem to internalize your statements and change their behavior in a form of self-fulfilling prophecy.

Where do you need some filler? Where do you need to move toward unity? Do you need to forgive someone? Do you need to ask for someone's forgiveness? Stop now and ask the Artist to help you do so. Start to fill the gap and advance the relationship today.

Try approaching someone you otherwise wouldn't and ask them to tell you the story behind their tattoo.

Reinking, Cover-ups, and Goo: Care and Maintenance of Your New Tattoo

Not that I have already obtained all this, or have already arrived at my goal, but I press on to take hold of that for which Christ Jesus took hold of me.

—Philippians 3:12 (NIV)

> *Your artist has done his best to build you a good tattoo, but remember it takes both of us to make the final job as perfect as it should be.*
>
> *—No. 6 of famous tattoo artist Sailor Jerry's Proper Care of Your New Tattoo instructions*

Despite baseball player Josh Hamilton's miraculous comeback, he's had a couple of widely publicized slipups. The particulars aren't important. As tattooist John Reardon said, "It is nearly impossible for the line of every tattoo a tattooist does to be utterly perfect. Every customer has a tendency to move now and again." It happens. And despite the Artist's work, we don't always do our part in the maintenance of our new tattoo.

How do we make the final job as perfect as it should be? How do we ensure that our new tattoo looks its best? What do we do when the ink hasn't held up? And what do we do when we realize we've inked a wrong tattoo altogether?

Defending Your Tattoo Against Foreign Objects

According to Reardon, how you care for your new tattoo will affect how it looks for the rest of your life, and the first thing he recommends is a bandage to protect it from dirt and foreign objects. Spiritually speaking, the apostle Paul wrote that our fight isn't really in the realm of flesh and blood, but that we're in a battle against forces of cosmic darkness. Josh Hamilton's struggle with those spiritual forces was blatantly displayed in demonic designs on his skin. Ours may be more covert but no less destructive.

Fortunately, our Artist provides a protective covering. When the apostle Paul wrote to put on God's armor so that we can take a stand against the devil's schemes, he described in detail the defensive protection for ink: a belt of truth, a breastplate of justice, shoes fitted with the gospel of peace, a shield of faith, and a helmet of salvation.

For starters, a belt holds up the whole armor. When Jesus said that he is the way, the truth, and the life, and no one comes to the Father except through him, he was saying that *he* is that belt of truth. We can be tempted to mix our inks—maybe a dab of this and a dab of that mixed in with our Jesus. But the minute we start to allow any false truths, any foreign objects, to creep in, we're in trouble.

Like a soldier's breastplate covering the vital organs from the neck to the thighs, we're covered by God's righteousness, a righteousness that Paul wrote comes from faith in Jesus Christ. Our feet are firmly rooted in the gospel to prevent us from slipping. We put on the

helmet of salvation and take up the shield of faith, Paul wrote, so that we may "extinguish the flaming arrows of the evil one." As believers, we're already wearing this armor. But that doesn't mean some foreign debris can't creep in and infect our spiritual tattoos. Fortunately for us, a healing balm is available.

Tattoo Goo

When Jeremiah the prophet mourned that the people of God were broken because of their sins, the Hebrew word he used for "broken" was *sheber,* meaning a "breaking," "fracture," "breach," or "crash." When we've sinned, don't we feel the crash? Whether it's a fracture in our relationship with God or with others, it can bring us to our knees.

Josh Hamilton knew what it was to have been redeemed from the pit. Because for a time, debris was able to get through his armor. "The great thing about a personal relationship with the Lord is that he keeps you strong," he said.

> But if you take your eyes off him, you fall back into the flesh and the world. He makes me strong every day, but once your priorities get out of whack, it doesn't take long to fall back into the flesh and the world. I got away from the one thing that kept me on the straight and narrow and that was my relationship with the Lord. That should always come first.

For all of us who have experienced a fracture in our relationship with the Lord or with others and have cried out for relief, there's a healing balm. The balm Jeremiah spoke of, the balm of Gilead, was a resin that was secreted from a tree that grew in Gilead. It was said to be worth twice its weight in silver for its healing properties. But a tree on Calvary produced our spiritual healing balm, and its worth is priceless. "Silver or gold I do not have," said the apostle Peter to a man crippled from birth, "but what I do have I give you. In the name of Jesus Christ of Nazareth, walk."

Jesus Christ is our Balm of Gilead, and our Artist says the healing ointment should be applied morning and night. King David wrote that it's good to proclaim God's love in the morning and his faithfulness at night. He said with confidence that when he laid it all out before God in the morning, he knew the Lord heard his voice and then he waited expectantly for the Lord's response. When we put God first and spend quality time with Him each day, He's able to protect what He's inked onto our hearts, and heal whatever is not from Him.

Besides the need to protect tattoos from foreign debris, John Reardon advises that you moisturize it regularly to help it heal and keep it in good condition. But rather than the balm Tattoo Goo, we have the balm of Gilead. And we apply it with those two offensive weapons the apostle Paul wrote about: the sword of the Spirit (the word of God) and prayer.

Norman Vincent Peale said, "That which the mind receives upon awakening tends to influence and, to a considerable degree, determine what your day will be." When our first moments of the day are spent talking with God and hearing back from Him by reading His word, we develop a sensitivity to what God is up to.

Turning Up the Heat

Besides using a protective covering and Tattoo Goo, John Reardon recommends another technique that can help the healing of your tattoo:

> While you are washing your tattoo, you will notice that it feels like a sunburn and is very sensitive to warm water. Let the warm water run over your fresh tattoo until the tattoo gets used to the temperature of the water. Once the water doesn't burn, turn up the temperature just a little so it irritates the tattoo again. Repeat this until the temperature of the water is just a little hotter than what you would consider a hot shower. This process will open the pores in the skin of your tattoo and wash out all of the dirt and excess ink.

Turning up the heat on our spiritual ink also has long-lasting benefits. Paul wrote that these "light and momentary troubles are achieving for us an eternal glory that far outweighs them all." The apostle James wrote that we should be joyful when we face various tests, because those tests of our faith produce endurance; and that endurance, when it finishes its work, leads to our maturity.

When Paul and James wrote of troubles, they were referring to hunger, persecution, scourging, imprisonment, and even death. What is it for you? Is it, like with Josh Hamilton, the fighting of an addiction? Have you been ridiculed or been passed over for opportunities because of your faith? Have you been tempted to doubt God's goodness because of trials? Have circumstances caused you to question the reality of God altogether, or that God cares for you?

Whatever it is for each of us, Paul wrote that we can take pride in these trials because they produce endurance, which in turn produces character, which in turn produces hope. And we're not put to shame because of this hope, because God's love—God's ink—has been "poured out in our hearts." Our faith is proved genuine through these trials. The ink is more deeply ingrained and reflects a glory to outshine all other ink.

Whatever we suffer for our faith, we know that these "light and momentary troubles" help our ink take hold and prevent it from fading.

Holidays

In tattoo lingo, once the ink is healed, "holidays" are spots of bare skin that pop through, revealing places where the ink didn't hold. You might say Josh Hamilton took a couple of "holidays" during his slipups.

There are really two types of holidays that take our minds off the Artist's work on our lives and leave bare spots in our design. When we focus on regrets, we're taking a mental vacation back to the past. Like Lot's wife, who despite God's command looked back on Sodom and turned into a pillar of salt, regret paralyzes us by keeping us in the past. And when we focus on worry and fears, we're taking a mental vacation into the future.

What regrets keep us in the past? When we confess our sins, the apostle John wrote that God will "cleanse us from everything we've done wrong," and the prophet Isaiah wrote that God blots out our sins and remembers them no more. When we pick at the scabs of our own sins or continue to nurse old wounds caused by others long after God has forgiven, we let the past define us. We run the risk of scarring. Confess, repent, and move on!

The emotion that keeps us stuck in the future is fear, also called worry or anxiety. How much of our thought life is preoccupied with the future? Our friend Sylva wrote this when she was in college:

> *Everyone is serving the grades and careers and "future" instead of serving God and allowing Him to take care of the other things. I've been struggling, too, with buying into their hierarchy of priorities. There's a big temptation to see college as this sort of parenthesis in life, like the mistakes we make now won't count in the long run. But it's destructive thinking because who I am now is who I'm going to be. I won't magically have achieved whatever it is I hope to have achieved (which is really just*

accolades in the eyes of man), and it's like Galatians 1:10: Am I now trying to win the approval of men, or of God? Or am I trying to please men? If I were still trying to please men, I would not be a servant of Christ. And I realized that I haven't been serving Christ, because I've been in the service of my own idea of success.

We can relate. We often miss out on life because we're so focused on getting to the next thing we need to do—get to college, get *through* college, get a job, get married, get our *kids* through college, *retire*. Jesus knew our tendency to fret about the future, and so he said:

> Don't worry about your life, what you'll eat or what you'll drink, or about your body, what you'll wear. Isn't life more than food and the body more than clothes? Look at the birds in the sky. They don't sow seed or harvest grain or gather crops into barns. Yet your heavenly Father feeds them. Aren't you worth much more than they are? Who among you by worrying can add a single moment to your life? . . . Instead, desire first and foremost God's kingdom and God's righteousness, and all these things will be given to you as well. Therefore, stop worrying about tomorrow, because tomorrow will worry about itself.

We fear rejection, criticism, losing a loved one, failure, growing old, and the list goes on. What can you add to the list?

Along with the spirit of despair and the spirit of falsehood,

the Bible says there's such a thing as a spirit of fear that torments our minds: "For God has not given us a spirit of fear, but of power and of love and of a *sound mind*." The word *worry* comes from the old Anglo-Saxon verb *wyrgan*, meaning "to choke or strangle," and that's exactly what the Scratcher does when he inflicts a spirit of fear. If he can ink on us worry about the future, he chokes off our ability to affect the present.

The Scratcher can also make sure we miss out on some pretty big adventures. For example, while learning to ride a bike, after repeated nosedives, Kim just knew she would be the only kid in history who couldn't ride a bike. And, the night before her first day of high school, she sat at her mother's feet crying that someone had made a mistake; she wasn't really as smart as the other kids—she must have somehow fooled everyone into thinking she deserved to be promoted to the ninth grade. Even into adulthood, she's always battled fear and the insecurity that she's not the one for the job.

And to this day, when she's standing in line for a roller-coaster ride, the thought enters her mind: "I'm going to be that one person you hear about where the screw comes loose and my car goes flying out into the crowd and I die." But her desire not to look like a freak in front of her friends forces her to face her fear, get in line, and talk incessantly about anything else to keep her mind off of it until she's at the front of the line and has no choice. The thought of the humiliation of walking down the stairs and past the long line of people at that point is worse than her fear.

What adventures does the Scratcher deny us by keeping us in

the future instead of in the here and now? And how do we master our fear?

The most repeated commandment in the Bible is "Fear not." Remember the biblical antidote to this Scratcher tactic? "Don't be anxious about anything; rather bring up all of your requests to God in your prayers and petitions, along with giving thanks. Then the peace of God that exceeds all understanding will keep your hearts and minds safe in Christ Jesus."

When Janet was eleven years old, doctors thought she might have cancer. She had to have major surgery for biopsies and remembers feeling anxious—until her mom said, "Why don't you let Dad carry you into the hospital?" She still remembers her dad's strong arms wrapped around her as he carried her up the long set of stairs and through the hospital doors. Even though a scary experience awaited her, the love and security she felt in her father's embrace brought trust and peace. In the same way, God carries us through our fears and we can trust him for the outcome.

Sometimes we take holidays. And sometimes our tattoos simply fade over time from neglect. We start to take them for granted. When holidays and fading have rendered our tattoos indistinct, there's only one thing to do. We go back to the Artist for some reinking.

In *God's Psychiatry*, Charles Allen explains that the word *psychiatry* comes from two Greek words: *psyche* ("soul" or "mind") and *iatreia* ("treatment," "healing," or "restoring"). In other words, the healing of the mind or a restoring of the soul. In fact, in the twenty-third Psalm, King David wrote that God restored his soul and, later in the Psalms, he wrote that he would remember the Lord's deeds and his wondrous acts from long ago.

What holidays have you taken from the tattoo God wants displayed in your life now? Are there parts of God's word you would prefer to ignore? Are you hearing promptings from God that are especially hard for you to ink? If so, heed a caution from *The Complete Idiot's Guide to Getting a Tattoo*: "The longer the break you take, the more it hurts when you start again because you have to get used to the feeling again." When you need some reinking, go to the Artist, confess your sins, tell Him about your fears, remember what He has already done, and let Him restore your soul.

Cover-ups

We've all heard a version of it—the "morning after" tattoo story. A guy indulges a little too much at the bar and, in his drunkenness, decides Stephanie is *the* one and gets her name tattooed across his chest. The sun rises, the fog clears, and he's left considering whether to change his name to Stefano with a *ph*.

Sometimes we take holidays and sometimes the ink fades, but what if we realize we've just plain allowed some bad art to be tattooed on us? There's always laser removal as an option, but as the actor Mark Wahlberg found out, it's expensive, it's very painful, it takes quite a few sessions, it may not be totally effective, and it may leave scarring. In an interview on *The Tonight Show*, Wahlberg said he was in the process of having all of his tattoos removed now that he's a father of four and desiring to erase the evidence of his former bad-boy image.

He described the removal process like this:

> When I started removing them, they said it'd take five to seven visits. I'd been twenty-something times and I took my two oldest to watch because it's like getting burnt with hot bacon grease, there's blood coming up, it looks like somebody welded your skin, there's these welts that come up like a quarter of an inch. Hopefully that will deter them from getting (tattoos).

Ouch. For Wahlberg and anyone else who's so ashamed of their tattoos that they're willing to endure the equivalent of being burned with hot bacon grease, do we have some good news for you. Jesus already suffered for your mistakes. Only instead of being expensive, it's a free gift of God; instead of requiring a few sessions, Jesus' sacrifice was final; and instead of leaving any reminders of the old behind, he completely saves those who approach God through him.

Jesus already endured the pain on our behalf. He doesn't remove our past; he covers it. Sometimes, instead of laser removal, artists will recommend that it is much easier to cover an old, undesired tattoo with new art. Just as Josh has discovered that God can use his tattoos as an opening to tell his story, just as Pete covered his old identity with a picture of the cross, and just as Lilly covered her old identity with a flower to signify beauty from ashes, God will use every part of who *you* are to reach others.

God's grace is sufficient because God's power is made perfect in weakness, and the apostle Paul said that he would therefore boast all the more gladly about his weaknesses, so that Christ's power would rest on him. John Reardon writes, "Drawing a cover-up so an old tattoo is 'gone' takes an immense amount of work and concentration. This is where tattooing becomes more of an art than a craft." And as we've seen, we *are* his masterpiece.

Never Mind How It Will Look When You're Eighty

In the fall of 1991, Erika and Helmut Simon of Germany were hiking the Ötztal Alps in Italy when they left the marked trail for a shortcut. They soon discovered, to their horror, a human corpse lying facedown in the glacier's meltwater.

Archaeologists have determined that "Ötzi the Iceman" lived between 3350 and 3100 B.C. and had been preserved for more than five thousand years by ice, making him Europe's oldest natural human mummy. Scientists have discovered some interesting bits of information about Ötzi, who with his personal belongings is on display at the South Tyrol Museum of Archaeology in Italy.

He was around five foot three, weighed approximately 110 pounds, and had dark wavy hair, a beard, and brown eyes; was missing a pair of ribs; suffered from hardened arteries, whipworm, and a chronic illness; probably spent a lot of time around open fires (his lungs were black); was a meat-and-potatoes kind of guy (or at least meat and some kind of vegetables, as evidenced by the contents in his stomach); was involved in hand-to-hand combat before suffering what was probably the fatal wound of an arrowhead through his left shoulder; sported a striped goatskin coat, loincloth, bearskin cap, bear- and deerskin shoes, and the oldest known pair of leggings; and carried a pouch that held tools for sewing and making fires, an ax, a dagger, a bow, quiver and arrows, and even a first-aid kit!

But are you ready for the kicker? Ötzi had more than fifty tattoos! Groups of lines and crosses were fashioned by rubbing charcoal into fine cuts in his skin.

It just goes to show how the proper care and maintenance of your tattoo can affect how it will look for many years to come. Sure, that pinup girl on your bicep or the butterfly on your thigh may look a little distorted by the time you're getting sponge baths in the nursing home, but how will your figurative tattoos—your spiritual legacy—be recognized long after you're gone? If you preserve them now and take care in passing them on to the next generation, you'll affect the world way more than in just teaching future generations what we wore, ate, and how we died. How many generations might learn of the Word Made Flesh by your testimony?

Engrave It!

What foreign objects or debris have threatened the integrity of your tattoo? What part of the armor have you neglected? Go to the healing Balm of Gilead in confession and prayer. If you aren't in the habit of spending time with him both morning and night, try starting with fifteen minutes in the morning and fifteen minutes before bedtime. It's been said that it takes thirty days to develop a habit, but don't beat yourself up if you miss a morning. Perfection isn't the goal here: effort and quality time with your Artist is. The nineteenth-century philosopher William Hazlitt said, "Great thoughts reduced to practice become great acts." Who knows what great acts might come from this practice?

Think back on the events and conversations of the day. Did you act in disobedience? Confess and ask God's forgiveness. Did you do or say something hurtful to another? Determine to make amends tomorrow. Then determine to do what Paul the apostle did: forget about the things that are behind you and reach out for what is ahead.

The psalmist wrote that he remembered the days long past, that he meditated on all God's deeds and contemplated His handiwork. Make a list of all of the trials you have experienced, times in your life where the heat has been turned up. For each one, list all the ways that God used those events to His glory. Was your testimony strengthened? Were you able to comfort another because of your experience? Did you receive blessings or opportunities for growth? Thank God.

Indelible

Jesus Christ is the same yesterday, today and forever!

—Hebrews 13:8

Tattoo: n. an indelible mark or figure fixed upon the body by insertion of pigment under the skin or by production of scars.

Ellen is the essence of innocence. With big hazel-green eyes and unruly curly ringlets, she has the face of a cherub and a voice that causes callers to ask this twenty-something if they can speak with her mommy or daddy. But in Ellen's short life, she's already been on several international mission trips, worked with at-risk youth in the United States and Canada, and been the hands and feet of Jesus to drug addicts, the homeless, gang members, prisoners, and prostitutes.

Her reputation for being a walking showcase for God is known even among strangers. One night, while walking home, she was approached by a taxi driver who yelled, "Hey, aren't you that Christian girl?!"

But just in case there's ever any question, she has tattooed on her arm in Amharic, the language spoken in her husband's home country of Ethiopia, the words "I belong to the Lord." They reference a passage in the book of Isaiah, where God tells Israel that He is going to pour out His Spirit on her descendants and that "some will say, 'I belong to the LORD'"; and "still others will write on their hand, 'The LORD's.'"

One commentator writes that this referred to marks

> made by punctures rendered indelible, by fire or by staining, upon the hand or some other part of the body, signifying the state or character of the person, and to whom he belonged. The

slave was marked with the name of the master; the soldier, of his commander; the idolater, with the name or ensign of his god."

He goes on to say that Christians seem to have imitated this practice, based on what the sixth-century historian Procopius wrote: "Many marked their wrists, or their arms, with the sign of the cross, or with the name of Christ.

There's an interesting prophecy in the Old Testament that tells of a man clothed in linen (in Revelation 19:8 in the New Testament, fine linen symbolizes righteousness or acts of justice) who has a writing kit at his side. God calls to him to go throughout the city of Jerusalem and to put a mark on the foreheads of those who grieved over all the detestable things that were done in the city. Scholars believe this man is an Old Testament reference to Christ serving as mediator, saving the remnant in Jerusalem from the ultimate destruction that was to occur there.

In Isaiah, God tells His people that He has inscribed them onto the palms of His hands and that Jerusalem's walls are ever before Him. The New International Version translates the original Hebrew as "engraved," and *The Living Bible* says, "I have tattooed your name upon my palm." It's the same root word that is used in Proverbs to describe when God marked out the foundations of the earth.

One commentator said that it may be a reference to an architect's plans for a building, and that God had inscribed the plans for Jerusalem on his palm: "The idea is, that God had laid out the plan of Jerusalem long before it was built, and that it was so dear to him that he had even engraven it on his hands. . . . He had a

constant and sacred regard for his people, and amidst all their disasters and trials, still remembered them."

God said Jerusalem's walls were ever before him, even when it was destroyed in 586 B.C. by the Babylonians and again in A.D. 70 by the Romans. Of the A.D. 70 siege, the first-century Jewish historian Josephus wrote that it was now so unrecognizable that if a foreigner who had once before been to Jerusalem now happened upon it, he wouldn't even know it was the same city.

But God says that He has inscribed Jerusalem's walls on the palm of His hand. And, despite its destruction, the Old Testament foretells that God, out of His great love for His people, would save a remnant by having Christ the mediator mark the foreheads of the righteous.

Ellen has also experienced the destruction of her own plans. When Ellen says, "God is good," she doesn't say it flippantly as some might do after, say, finding a pair of coveted shoes on sale or hitting a string of green traffic lights. When Ellen says God is good, you can bet she has learned it by persevering through trials— which is how she came to get the tattoo on her ankle. A tree with curling branches and a colorful leaf here and there sprawls up from the words of Revelation 21:1-5: "He makes all things new."

Read Ellen's motivation, in her own words, for getting this tattoo:

> *My time as a missionary in Winnipeg had taught me that God makes all things new. It had become a very*

powerful, encouraging thing. It was how I understood my God as a God of love, even when mothers die and children are raised around drug addictions and teenagers are in prostitution. God makes all things new. He doesn't just fix what is broken, he brings NEW life to what is dead.

When I transferred to a new school to finish my degree, I immediately fell in love with the school. I was on the soccer team, I was studying my passion, I had great roommates and was enjoying my college life. A month into the semester, the campus announced that it was closing. Students were advised to either transfer to another campus with the same college (that didn't offer the degree I was studying) or transfer to a new college. Everything that I had planned for my future changed. God reminded me that he makes all things new. He can (and DOES!) turn bad situations into good. What is dead he can bring life to.

A few months after I got married, I woke up to a phone call that my husband was hurt. He had been stabbed multiple times, and nearly died. Immediate surgery saved his life; but life would not return to normal. He couldn't return to work, so he decided to open his own business. Starting a business was hard, certainly. But the real struggle was that my husband suffered from post-traumatic stress, constant underlying anger, nightmares, and living his life in fear.

I was struggling, too. I remember praying to God and describing that I felt as if my life had been bombed; buildings crumbling, destroyed, smoke rising from the rubble. I felt like that for a long time. After sharing my feelings with friends at church, one prayed for me and described a picture that came to her mind while she was praying for me: a beautiful forest, full of sunlight. I had imagined that my life, as a city, had been bombed and destroyed and that it needed

rebuilding. But God didn't want to rebuild my life, he wanted to give me a NEW life. And that—that promise of new—is so much more powerful and hopeful than repairing something thatis broken.

I've wanted this tattoo for a while, because the verse from Revelation talks about the New Jerusalem and how God promises to take away all fear and sadness and to make all things new. There is one green leaf on my tree—as in the tree was dying, but God is making it new. And throughout my life, as God moves, as he makes me new, as he carries me through hard stuff, I will add more leaves on to the tree so one day, as I'm old, I'll look at the green leaves covering the tree and remember that God is good.

I see it as the foundation of my entire faith: that God makes people new. From the first conversation with Jesus, he doesn't just promise you a better life or a more fulfilling life in him. He promises a NEW life, a rebirth.

Ellen's words sound remarkably similar to the apostle Paul's when he wrote, "Even if our bodies are breaking down on the outside, the person that we are on the inside is being renewed every day." In fact, Ellen has since added two more leaves to her tattoo to symbolize continued renewal in her life.

Paul said, "Our temporary minor problems are producing an eternal stockpile of glory for us that is beyond all comparison. We don't focus on the things that can be seen but on the things that can't be seen. The things that can be seen don't last, but the things that can't be seen are eternal."

All of this brings us back to the garden of Eden. Next to the tree of the knowledge of good and evil was the tree of life. Throughout history, God has said to his people, "I have set before you life and death, blessings and curses." Sin entered this world, but in the words of the apostle Peter, Christ "bore our sins in his body on the tree, so that we might die to sins and live for righteousness." And choosing Christ, the book of Revelation says, means we'll live in an eternal city where that tree of life still grows.

A tattoo is defined as an indelible mark on the skin. But the fact is, tattoos can be changed. Thankfully, the God "who was and is and is coming" provided a way to change the mental ink we regret. It doesn't have to be indelible. None of us get out of this world without being marked by something. The remarkable thing is that we choose what that will be.

Neuroscience is proving that our brains are not static—we can be transformed by the renewing of our minds. Science has conceded that God *does* change our brains. But many wonder if it's our brains that have created God, rather than the other way around. After all, they say, it doesn't matter *which* god is the object of our meditation. The benefits, they say, are the same. But remember, that's one of the Scratcher's oldest lies—the lie about *your true Artist.*

God is not *our* inkling; we are His. He is not inked in our image. He allows us to be active participants in our design, but we are His creation, custom work made in His image. And He has promised not to abandon the works of His hand.

In the epilogue to *How God Changes Your Brain*, Dr. Andrew Newberg attempts to answer the question of whether he personally believes God is real. He describes how he has contemplated God since he was a child and has come to view God's relationship to man as a metaphorical analogy to man's relationship to his dog. As our lives are profoundly more complex than a dog's, he said, so is God's existence more complex than ours.

Inasmuch as we believe God to be omniscient and infinite, he continued, we can no more grasp God's thoughts than a dog can understand anything more than his name and some basic commands from us. Newberg said that even if we believe that the Scriptures are the word of God, it's impossible for imperfect human beings to fully know God's thoughts or to fully capture who God is. He'll get no argument from us there. The psalmist wrote, "God, your plans are incomprehensible to me! Their total number is countless! If I tried to count them—they outnumber grains of sand!"

But we depart from Newberg's analogy on two points. First, unlike a dog to a man, God created us and we are made in God's image. Whether or not you believe those two points is really important. Remember, the second primary tactic of the Scratcher is the lie about *who you are*. If you believe that you are to God as a dog is to a man and not made in the image of God, then there are all kinds of earthly and eternal ramifications.

Second, we cannot possibly completely understand God (what kind of God would that be?), but we can *know* God. He sent his Son so that we can know him, for Jesus Christ has said, "I am the way, the the truth, and the life. No one comes to the Father except through me. If you have really known me, you will also know the Father."

Even Newberg admits that this is where faith steps in. As a physician, he said he has faith, not certainty, in medical treatments and that he believes his patients' faith betters their odds for success.

Throughout this book, we've used tattoo culture as a metaphor to describe how Christ is able to radically change the marks made on our minds and on our lives. He is the Word that "became flesh and made his home among us," and we have seen his glory. To borrow the tagline for the tattoo competition TV series *Ink Master,* "This is where the stakes are high and the mistakes are permanent." Who do *you* say Jesus is?

Only Jesus is indelible—"the same yesterday, today and forever." He was pierced and shed very real blood and died a brutal death on the cross so that we *can* change. Who we've *been*, or who we *are*, is not who we have to *be*. He is making all things new. In Revelation 3:12, Jesus says, "As for those who emerge victorious, I will make them pillars in the temple of my God, and they will never leave it. I will write on them the name of my God and the name of the city of my God, the New Jerusalem that comes down out of heaven from my God. I will also write on them my own new name."

There is only one tattoo that really counts, only one that is indelible. Jesus has the ultimate victory over the Scratcher, and on his thigh is this tattoo: "King of kings and Lord of lords."

Is he *your* King and Lord? Because, in the end, that's the only thing that's tattoo worthy.

There will no longer be any curse. The throne of God and the Lamb will be in it, and his servants will worship him. They will see his face, and his name will be on their foreheads. Night will be no more. They won't need the light of a lamp or the light of the sun, for the Lord God will shine on them, and they will rule forever and always.
—Revelation 22:3-5

Engrave It!

Perhaps you've never thought of yourself as custom work created by a Master Artist. Maybe you've allowed the Scratcher to hack the wrong messages into your life for far too long. If so, get in the chair! Confess the toxic ink that you've been showcasing, and allow the Master Artist to do His work on you so that you become a showcase for God's glory. Allow God to penetrate you with the double-edged sword of His word and join a community of others who have been inked by the Word Made Flesh.

We’d love to hear from you!

To read more stories of transformation or to share your own, visit us at www.InkedbyGod.com.

We are two works in progress who owe everything to the Artist who introduced us long ago. To God, the designer of our lives, who is infinitely patient with us when we wrastle in the chair. Our hearts' desire is that we would be His showcases.

We are additionally grateful to the following people:

John Robertson at Sherwood Oaks Christian Church—for giving us the idea to use tattoo as metaphor in your sermon "Every Tattoo Tells a Story."

Our agent, Tim Beals, with Credo Communications, LLC—for your wisdom and guidance.

Lil Copan, Pamela Clements and the team at Abingdon Press—for believing in this project.

Sarah Baar, our editor—for your hard work and gentleness in skillfully reinking our scratches.

Stephanie Reeves at Spectrum Studio and Rick Schroeppel at Abingdon Press—for representing our thoughts with your creative designs.

Sylva Johnson, Ellen Pashley, Nick Childress, Matthew Childress, and Cynthia Childress—for your early review of the manuscript and valuable feedback.

Lillian Shelton—for inviting us to a chair-side experience of your tattoo. Way to take one for the team!

Finally, to Josh Hamilton and all the rest who bravely shared your stories, thank you.

Introduction: Words Become Flesh

Please note that many names have been changed throughout the book to protect the individuals' identities and privacy.

An estimated 45 million Americans . . . stories.
From a Food and Drug Administration report, cited in "Tattoos," *New York Times*, February 2, 2012, http://topics.nytimes.com/top/reference/timestopics/subjects/t/tattoos/index.html.

Bulleted list from American College Health Association National College Health Assessment II, Spring 2011 Reference Group Summary, www.achancha.org/docs/ACHA-NCHA-II_ReferenceGroup_ExecutiveSummary_Spring2011.pdf.

"Everything can be taken from a man . . . own way."
Viktor Frankl, *Man's Search for Meaning* (New York: Washington Square Press, 1984), 86.

During the time of Roman emperor Nero's . . . minds.
See Romans 12:2.

"The Word became flesh and made his home among us."
John 1:14.

"Don't cause me any grief about this . . . marks of Jesus."
Author interpretation of Galatians 6:15, 17.

"God is less interested . . . hearts are tough."
Louie Giglio, *Tattoo* (Roswell, Ga.: Passion Conferences, 2006), DVD.

1. Showcases: Choosing Your Artist

According to the Pew Research Center, . . . one tattoo.
Adam Kent Isaac, "Bloomington Ink," *Bloom Magazine*, October/November 2010, 86–95.

But long before the star outfielder . . . play baseball.
Albert Chen, "The Super Natural," SI Vault, June 2, 2008, http://sportsillustrated.cnn.com/vault/article/magazine/MAG1138934/index.htm.

Josh would spend hours in the chair . . . skin-deep.
Hamilton, *Beyond Belief*, 69, 71.

"The land we explored devours those living in it. . . . same to them."
Numbers 13:27-28, 30, 32-33 (NIV).

The Bible says we are "God's handiwork," . . . "his splendor."
Ephesians 2:10; Isaiah 64:8; and Isaiah 61:3 (NIV).

"The truth is, most of the time . . . were in charge."
Hamilton, *Beyond Belief*, 73–74.

He said that what started out . . . master to obey.
Hamilton, *Beyond Belief*, 72.

"There was lightning in the distance. . . . There was something there for me, some message or warning."
Hamilton, *Beyond Belief*, 52.

What he saw . . . "respond to His message."
Hamilton, *Beyond Belief*, 52–53.

"I was a bad husband. . . . Baseball wasn't even on my mind."
Evan Grant, "Faith Brings Texas Rangers' Hamilton Back from the Brink," *Dallas Morning News*, February 29, 2008, http://dallasnews.com.

"I'm tired of you killing yourself. . . . people who care about you."
Grant, "Faith Brings Texas Rangers' Hamilton Back."

"I was fighting the devil. . . . crawled under the covers with her."
Josh Hamilton (as told to Tim Keown), "I'm Proof That Hope Is Never Lost," *ESPN The Magazine*, July 16, 2007, http://sports.espn.go.com/mlb/news/story?id=2926447.

"Submit yourselves, then, to God. Resist the devil, and he will flee from you."
James 4:7 (NIV).

"The devil stayed out of my dreams . . . my marriage and my life back together."
Hamilton, "I'm Proof That Hope Is Never Lost."

Josh desperately wanted . . . that meant he'd get back to playing ball.
Hamilton, *Beyond Belief*, 167–69.

"I would hit him and he would bounce back up . . . With Jesus, I couldn't lose."
Hamilton, "I'm Proof That Hope Is Never Lost."

"The LORD is with you, mighty warrior!"
Judges 6:12.

What do you mean . . . least in my family!"
See Judges 6:13-15.

"calls things that don't exist into existence."
Romans 4:17.

"Addiction is a humbling experience. . . . That didn't work out so well."
Hamilton, "I'm Proof That Hope Is Never Lost."

There was yet another . . . and his weapon was a slingshot.
1 Samuel 17.

"I just got this big grin on my face and said that it has been sharing Christ with millions of people."
Josh Hamilton in telephone discussion with authors, October 5, 2009.

"He's not worried about accolades, . . . I glorify Him in everything I do."
Josh Hamilton, interview on *Larry King Live*, available on www.you tube.com/watch?v=rJ2xN_xHT0g&feature=related.

"This may sound crazy, . . . Believe me, I know."
Hamilton, "I'm Proof That Hope Is Never Lost."

"If I had stayed that clean-cut kid, . . . They're my battle scars."
Josh Hamilton in telephone discussion with the authors, October 5, 2009.

"I will become whatever image I hold of myself and life, and therefore I will picture what I can be when filled with the Lord's power."
Lloyd John Ogilvie, *God's Best for My Life* (Eugene, Ore.: Harvest House, 1981), 295.

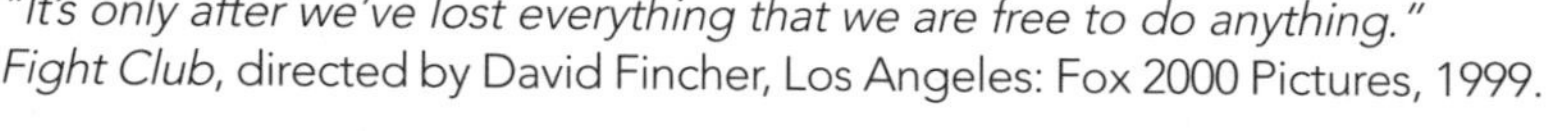

2. Flash vs. Custom: Choosing the Tattoo Worthy

"It's only after we've lost everything that we are free to do anything."
Fight Club, directed by David Fincher, Los Angeles: Fox 2000 Pictures, 1999.

"One question about your business, . . . No worries then."
Pirates of the Caribbean: The Curse of the Black Pearl, directed by Gore Verbinski, Burbank: Walt Disney Pictures, 2003.

They include penicillin . . . and the first toilet paper on a roll!
See "A Guide to Inventions and Discoveries from Adrenaline to the Zipper" at www.infoplease.com.

"I want you to know that the things . . . or whether having plenty or being poor."
Philippians 1:12; 4:11-12.

"think about the things above and not things on earth."
Colossians 3:2.

Marked by business failure . . . president in 1860.
Alan Loy McGinnis, *Bringing Out the Best in People* (Minneapolis: Augsburg, 1985), 76.

"I want it said . . . flower would grow.
http://www.brainyquote.com/quotes/quotes/a/abrahamlin161523.html

"They may have been few in number . . . to choose one's own way."
Frankl, *Man's Search for Meaning*, 86.

"Only through experiences . . . and success achieved."
http://en.thinkexist.com/quotes/helen_keller/2.html

"You may not realize it . . . best thing in the world for you."
www.brainyquote.com/quotes/authors/w/walt_disney.html

"You planned something bad for me . . . in order to save the lives of many people."
Genesis 50:20.

"I have earned the secret . . . situation."
Philippians 4:12 (NIV)

"I can endure all these things through the power of the one who gives me strength."
Philippians 4:13.

He's an Artist who numbers the hairs on our heads.
Luke 12:7.

who records our every tear
Psalm 56:8.

who perceives our thoughts . . . before they even leave our mouths
Psalm 139:4.

who set us apart before we were born
Jeremiah 1:5.

This is the Artist who says we are a masterpiece.
Ephesians 2:10 (NLT).

"Do not conform . . . by the renewing of your mind."
Romans 12:2.

"Whatever is true, whatever is noble, . . . the God of peace will be with you."
Philippians 4:8-9 (NIV).

Norman Vincent Peale, *The Power of Positive Thinking*, First Fireside ed. (New York: Simon & Schuster, 2003).

The thought must be replaced by something positive.
Alison Wellner and David Adox, "Happy Days," *Psychology Today*, May/June 2000, 32–37.

At the least, he advises compartmentalizing the time we spend sending and receiving electronic messages.
"Tweeting Hazard: New Study Warns of Twitter Dangers," www.foxnews.com/health. An interview by Martha MacCallum of Fox News's *The Live Desk* with Dr. Marty Makary from Johns Hopkins.

"healing balm for the emotional hardships."
Richard Louv, *Last Child in the Woods* (Chapel Hill, N.C.: Algonquin Books, 2005), 47.

"Stop and consider God's wonders."
Job 37:14 (NIV).

Proving the proverb that a joyful heart helps healing, . . .
Proverbs 17:22.

According to Dr. Caroline Leaf, . . . endorphin by 29 percent.
Caroline Leaf, *Who Switched Off My Brain?* (Dallas: Switch On Your Brain, 2007), 128–29.

"It is well-known that humor, . . . even if only for a few seconds."
Frankl, *Man's Search for Meaning*, 63.

But long before these men acknowledged . . . made new in the attitude of our minds.
Ephesians 4:23 (NIV).

3. Scratcher Tactics: Beware the Hacker

"an unskilled artist who causes more pain and swelling than necessary."
http://mag.rankmytattoos.com/ultimate-guide-to-tattoo-and-piercing-slang.html.

Jesus called the Scratcher the father of lies.
John 8:44.

"You won't die! . . . you will be like God."
Genesis 3:4-5.

"For the wages of sin is death, but the gift of God is eternal life in Christ Jesus our Lord."
Romans 6:23 (NKJV).

"This is my Son whom I dearly love; I find happiness in him."
Matthew 3:17.

"If you are the Son of God, tell these stones to become bread."
Matthew 4:3 (NIV).

"Since you are God's Son, . . . so that you won't hit your foot on a stone."
Matthew 4:6.

"I'll give you . . . and worship me."
Matthew 4:9.

"In each case the appeal was a real appeal . . . can give the help needed by the fallen."
F. L. Anderson, "Temptation of Christ," http://classic.net.bible.org/dictionary.php?word=Temptation%20Of%20Christ.

"'He himself bore our sins' . . . for righteousness."
1 Peter 2:24 (NIV).

"Very truly I tell you . . . before Abraham was born, I am!"
John 8:58 (NIV).

"'I am the Alpha and the Omega,' . . . the Almighty.'"
Revelation 1:8.

But Jesus Christ came to give us abundant life.
John 10:10.

List adapted from David D. Burns, *The Feeling Good Handbook* (New York: Penguin, 1999), 96.

"We need to learn to love the flawed, . . . for creating them."
http://www.ted.com/talks/kathryn_schulz_don_t_regret_regret.html.

"looking out the window, wishing I was somewhere else."
http://www.squidoo.com/angelina_jolie_tattoos.

"I put my guard up so hard. . . . I put that up until it felt real."
Josh Eells, "Queen of Pain," *Rolling Stone* no. 1128:40–80, Academic Search Premier, EBSCOhost.

Her tattoo artist, Keith "Bang Bang" McCurdy, said it's a symbol of "strength and power."
Keith "Bang Bang" McCurdy, quoted in Jocelyn Vena, "Rihanna Shows Off New Gun Tattoo," *MTV News,* March 26, 2009, http://www.mtv.com/news/articles/1607825/20090326/rihanna.jhtml.

"You pick out a single negative detail . . . you have blinders on."
Burns, *Feeling Good,* 96.

"Never a failure, always a lesson."
http://www.okmagazine.com/photos/hot-shots/photos-rihanna-inks-her-new-motto-her-chest, December 8, 2009, accessed December 11, 2011.

"When you exaggerate the importance . . . other fellow's imperfections).
Burns, *Feeling Good*, 96.

"We have this hope as an anchor for the soul, firm and secure."
Hebrews 6:19 (NIV).

Long before Katy Perry . . . on their wrists and foreheads.
Deuteronomy 6:4-8.

This time, God said He would imprint His law onto their minds and write it on their hearts.
Jeremiah 31:33.

And what ink machine did God use? Jesus.
Hebrews 12:24.

"The relationship between the person . . . you're trusting them to do it right."
Isaac, "Bloomington Ink," 86–95.

When the apostle Paul wrote . . . which is the Word of God.
Ephesians 6:17.

"guard your heart above everything else, for it determines the course of your life."
Proverbs 4:23 (NLT).

If we tend to disqualify the positive, . . . through him who gives us strength.
Philippians 4:12-13.

If we struggle . . . according to the grace given us.
Romans 12:3-6.

"Any thought that lasts for eight seconds . . . turning point in my life and recovery."
Josh Hamilton in telephone discussion with authors, October 5, 2009.

Besides developing an intimacy . . . Jesus also told his disciples to pray.
Mark 14:38.

"Tattoo equipment is very sacred to a tattooist. . . . how well the tattoo will turn out."
John Reardon, *The Complete Idiot's Guide to Getting a Tattoo* (New York: Alpha Books, 2008), 67.

Prayer and the Scripture, Paul wrote, . . . them up with Christ.
2 Corinthians 10:3-5.

"Work with as little power . . . to use power when necessary."
www.tattooeducation.com/Ask_Guy/Ask_Guy_Aitchison.html.

"written not with ink . . . but on tablets of human hearts."
2 Corinthians 3:3 (NIV).

Symbolic to her that God does bring beauty out of ashes
Isaiah 61:3 (NIV).

"Our research team at the University of Pennsylvania . . . God can change your brain."
Andrew Newberg and Mark Robert Waldman, *How God Changes Your Brain: Breakthrough Findings from a Leading Neuroscientist* (New York: Ballantine, 2010), 4.

4. B-Backs and Wrastlers: Getting (and Staying) in the Chair

She still feels the sting of the mark . . . death has lost its sting
1 Corinthians 15:55.

"Good Teacher . . . And come, follow me."
Mark 10:17-22.

"Jesus looked at him carefully and loved him."
Mark 10:21.

"with minds that are alert . . . revealed at his coming"
1 Peter 1:13 (NIV).

Both used the typical argument . . . will never be able to throw away his life."
Frankl, *Man's Search for Meaning*, 100–101.

"Suddenly I saw myself standing . . . psychology of the concentration camp!"
Frankl, *Man's Search for Meaning*, 94–95.

"wept and begged for his favor."
Hosea 12:4 (NIV).

"I will not let you go . . . have overcome."
Genesis 32:26-28 (NIV).

And, like Jacob, after wrestling with God, . . . wherever she's gone.
Genesis 35:3.

"I forget about the things behind me . . . upward call in Christ Jesus."
Philippians 3:13-14.

"To become heavily tattooed . . . getting your work completed."
Reardon, *Complete Idiot's Guide to Getting a Tattoo*, 59.

"Therefore, brothers and sisters . . . think about Jesus."
Hebrews 3:1.

"he steadfastly set his face to go to Jerusalem."
Luke 9:51 (KJV).

"firmly determined to accomplish his design."
Adam Clarke, *Clarke's Commentary on the Bible*, http://biblecommenter.com/luke/9-51.htm.

"fix our eyes on Jesus, . . . at the right side of God's throne."
Hebrews 12:2.

Practice these steps for visualizing your achievement of the new design.
Adapted from Daryl E. Quick, *The Healing Journey* (Downers Grove, Ill.: InterVarsity, 1990).

5. Kickin' It into Third: Achieving the Desired Result

A few days later, Kim found herself at Metamorphosis (voted . . . Indianapolis),
Selected by voters in the 2009 TheIndyChannel.com A-List, http://wrtv.cityvoter.com/best/tattoo-and-piercing/beauty/indianapolis/slideshow/2009.

"Blessed be the Lord, . . . who made heaven and earth."
Psalm 124:6-8 (KJV).

"the disease of our age"
George Lincoln Walton, *Why Worry?* (Philadelphia: J. B. Lippincott, 1908), 296.

Nine out of ten of the most prescribed psychiatric drugs . . . two hundred million prescriptions.
Suzanne Labarre, "Prescription Drug Stats a Bitter Pill to Swallow," *Fast Company*, May 12, 2010, www.fastcompany.com/1645800/prescription-drug-stats-a-bitter-pill-to-swallow.

"Be joyful always; pray continually; give thanks in all circumstances, for this is God's will for you in Christ Jesus."
1 Thessalonians 5:16-18 (NIV 1984).

"Don't be conformed to the patterns . . . good and pleasing and mature."
Romans 12:2.

The Greek for "will" . . . His "best offer."
Strong's Concordance and *Helps Word Studies*, http://concordances.org/greek/2307.htm.

Though we may be sad and hurting, . . . forever to intercede for us.
Hebrews 7:25.

"Think of all the beauty that's still left in and around you and be happy."
Anne Frank, *The Diary of Anne Frank: The Revised Critical Edition*, ed. David Barnouw and Gerrold Van Der Stroom (New York: Doubleday, 2003), 542.

"We are experiencing all kinds of trouble, . . . but we aren't knocked out."
2 Corinthians 4:8-9.

"The joy of the LORD is my strength."
Nehemiah 8:10.

They write that active and positive . . . perception of reality.
Newberg and Waldman, *How God Changes Your Brain*, from the jacket.

"Don't be anxious about anything; . . . minds safe in Christ Jesus."
Philippians 4:6-7.

"When we read Scripture, . . . start thinking God thoughts."
Mark Batterson, *In a Pit with a Lion on a Snowy Day* (Colorado Springs: Multnomah, 2006), 134–35.

Like tattoos that remind the imprinted . . . keep praying for all believers.
Ephesians 6:18.

He loves to show us that His eyes are on us and His ears are open to our prayers.
1 Peter 3:12.

"Don't be anxious about anything; . . . hearts and minds safe in Christ Jesus."
Philippians 4:6-7.

"that he had a healthy body, . . . a lot of people trusted him."
Norman Vincent Peale, *Enthusiasm Makes the Difference* (Greenwich, Conn.: Fawcett, 1967), 32.

The apostle Paul wrote that we should always give thanks to God the Father for everything!
Ephesians 5:20.

"This is the day the LORD has made; we will rejoice and be glad in it."
Psalm 118:24 (NKJV).

6. The Look: Seeing Your Tat for the First Time

"I think back on that man, . . . and people just don't look that closely."
Julie H. Rose, "Why You Should Not Get a Tattoo," May 25, 2008, *Everything Is Interesting* blog, http://juliesayseverythingisinteresting.blogspot.com/2008/05/why-you-should-not-get-tattoo.html.

"Lord, you know all. . . . You must follow me."
See John 21:15-22 (NIV).

Our unique marks are to be appreciated in each other and used for the common good.
Romans 12:3-6.

"We all hear voices . . . to listen to."
A Beautiful Mind, directed by Ron Howard, Hollywood: Universal Pictures, 2002.

However, they say there's one factor that determines self-esteem 100 percent of the time: our thoughts.
Matthew McKay and Patrick Fanning, *Self-Esteem: A Proven Program of Cognitive Techniques for Assessing, Improving and Maintaining Your Self-Esteem* (Oakland: New Harbinger, 2000), 3.

"When you look at my body, you can see my memories."
Kat von D, *High Voltage Tattoo: The Autobiography of Kat von D* (New York: HarperCollins, 2009), front matter.

Even if she thinks she's doing a good job . . . rob her of peace and joy.
Leaf, *Who Switched Off My Brain?*, 80.

I must do well. You must treat me well. The world must be easy.
Interview with Albert Ellis, www.cbtrecovery.org/interviewalbertellis.htm.

"In real life, . . . has a negative effect on your health."
Leaf, *Who Switched Off My Brain?*, 109.

He said it's with those tools that we capture every thought to make it line up with Christ.
2 Corinthians 10:5.

"Who am I *without weightlifting? What is my identity?"*
Giff Reed, interview with Kim Goad, September 30, 2009.

With Scripture and prayer, . . . a broken spirit and a contrite heart.
Psalm 51:17 (NIV).

Pointing to the passage in Hebrews . . . receive mercy and grace when we need it,
Hebrews 4:16.

What we do know is that the Greek for "thorn" . . . an instrument producing pain.
Helps Word Studies, 2011 by Helps Ministries, Inc., http://concordances.org/greek/4647.htm.

"My grace is sufficient for you, for my power is made perfect in weakness."
2 Corinthians 12:9 (NIV).

After all, he's the one who said . . . bold and confident access to God.
Ephesians 3:12.

When he returned to camp, . . . so the people could look at him.
Exodus 34:29-35.

"We love because God first loved us,"
1 John 4:19.

There was one who was pierced . . . we are healed.
Isaiah 53:5 (KJV).

"In fact, what was glorious isn't glorious now, . . . the one that lasts!"
2 Corinthians 3:10-11.

"Where the Lord's Spirit is, . . . to the next degree of glory."
2 Corinthians 3:17-18.

7. Works in Progress: Meeting Others in the Tattoo Shop

Eric committed his life to Christ, . . . transform him by renewing his mind.
Romans 12:2.

"Never consider unclean what God has made pure."
Acts 10:15.

"I really am learning that God doesn't show partiality to one group of people over another."
Acts 10:34.

We say we believe we're all made . . . in God's likeness.
James 3:9.

"Humans see only what is visible to the eyes, but the L*ORD* *sees into the heart."*
1 Samuel 16:7.

We conveniently forget that we've all sinned and fall short of God's glory.
Romans 3:22-23.

"I pray they will be one, Father, . . . loved them just as you loved me."
John 17:21-23.

"After applying the tattoo, . . . to be presented to the Queen."
www.nisnews.nl/dossiers/royal_house/150604_1383.htm.

So when anthropologist Tricia Allen . . . as a tattooist rather than as an academic.
Body Art (A Windstar Production in association with Pangolin Pictures for TIC, 2000), VHS.

In a similar way, Jesus . . . emptied himself by becoming one of us.
Philippians 2:6-7.

Paul wrote that if we get any encouragement . . . in spirit and purpose.
Philippians 2:1-2.

In fact, he called love "the perfect bond of unity."
Colossians 3:14.

And, he said the Artist creates . . . that we will all reach unity.
Ephesians 4:1-13.

When Jesus said that the greatest commandment . . . love your neighbor,
Luke 10:27.

That addendum . . . "Go and do likewise."
Luke 10:25-37.

"When you start to have . . . . will often be very polite back to you."
Reardon, *The Complete Idiot's Guide to Getting a Tattoo*, 23.

After all, tattoos have been called one of the most democratic forms of expression.
Body Art, 2000.

It's been likened to both a bit in a horse's mouth, . . . able to move an entire ship.
James 3:3-4.

They had a pianist who was doing a beautiful job. . . . that God is a God of second chances.
As told by Tom Ellsworth, senior minister at Sherwood Oaks Christian Church (Bloomington, Indiana), in a sermon on January 4, 2004.

It's like when Harry Potter pretended . . . just helped his confidence.
Harry Potter and the Half-Blood Prince, directed by David Yates, Burbank: Warner Bros. Pictures, 2009.

"Do not let any unwholesome talk come out of your mouths, but only what is helpful for building others up."
Ephesians 4:29 (NIV).

The apostle James wrote that the tongue is a world of evil at work within us.
James 3:6.

"Who can measure the evils . . . face of human affairs!"
Barnes' Notes on the Bible, http://biblecommenter.com/james/3-6.htm.

"that points to feedback loops . . . and integrity of our thought life."
Leaf, *Who Switched Off My Brain?*, 72.

Gives new meaning to Jesus' words that what goes out of the mouth comes from the heart, doesn't it?
Matthew 15:18.

In Ina Saltz's photographic book of tattoos, . . . through the black ink? FORGIVEN.
Ina Saltz, *Body Type: Intimate Messages Etched in Flesh* (New York: Abrams, 2006), 74.

Three other photos in Saltz's book . . . for the rest of their lives.
Saltz, *Body Type*, 72–75.

Jesus says, "Don't judge, and you won't be judged. . . . portion you receive in return."
Luke 6:37-38.

He tells us that even if we're in the middle of offering worship . . . fill the void.
Matthew 5:23-24.

But the two reasons in the top ten . . . "didn't feel connected to the people in my church."
"Church Dropouts: How many leave church between ages 18-22 and why?" LifeWay Research, Spring 2000, www.slideshare.net/daverudd/church-dropouts-how-many-leave-church-and-why.

His hope in doing so . . . no longer do so.
Kate Shellnutt, "Tattoos spread Montrose church's Lenten message," February 23, 2012, www.chron.com/news/article/Montrose-church-spreading-its-message-through-3354183.php.

"Like one from whom men hide their faces, . . . smitten by him, and afflicted."
Isaiah 53:2-4 (NIV 1984).

8. Reinking, Cover-ups, and Goo

"It is nearly impossible for the line . . . now and again."
Reardon, *Complete Idiot's Guide to Getting a Tattoo*, 127.

According to Reardon, . . . foreign objects.
Reardon, *Complete Idiot's Guide to Getting a Tattoo*, 182.

Spiritually speaking, the apostle Paul . . . of cosmic darkness.
Ephesians 6:12.

When the apostle Paul wrote to put . . . helmet of salvation.
Ephesians 6:11.

When Jesus said that he is the way, . . . belt of truth.
John 14:6.

Like a soldier's breastplate covering . . . comes from faith in Jesus Christ.
Romans 3:22.

We put on the helmet of salvation . . . "extinguish the flaming arrows of the evil one."
Ephesians 6:16.

When Jeremiah the prophet . . . or "crash."
Jeremiah 8; http://biblesuite.com/hebrew/7667.htm.

Josh Hamilton knew what it was to have been redeemed. . . . "That should always come first."
Josh Hamilton in telephone discussion with authors, October 5, 2009.

The balm Jeremiah spoke of, the balm of Gilead, . . . grew in Gilead.
Jeremiah 8:22.

"Silver or gold I do not have, . . . Christ of Nazareth, walk."
Acts 3:6 (NIV).

King David wrote that it's good . . . faithfulness at night.
Psalm 92:2.

He said with confidence . . . expectantly for the Lord's response.
Psalm 5:3.

Besides the need to protect tattoos . . . keep it in good condition.
Reardon, *Complete Idiot's Guide to Getting a Tattoo*, 110.

And we apply it with those . . . (the word of God) and prayer.
Ephesians 6:17-18.

"That which the mind receives . . . your day will be."
Peale, *Enthusiasm Makes the Difference*, 27.

"While you are washing your tattoo, . . . all of the dirt and excess ink."
Reardon, *Complete Idiot's Guide to Getting a Tattoo*, 182–83.

Paul wrote that these "light and momentary . . . them all."
2 Corinthians 4:17 (NIV).

The apostle James wrote . . . leads to our maturity.
James 1:2-4.

Paul wrote that we can take pride . . . "poured out in our hearts."
Romans 5:3-5.

In tattoo lingo, once the ink is healed, . . . didn't hold.
Reardon, *Complete Idiot's Guide to Getting a Tattoo*, 175.

"cleanse us from everything we've done wrong,"
1 John 1:9.

the prophet Isaiah wrote that God blots out our sins and remembers them no more.
Isaiah 43:25.

"Don't worry about your life, . . . because tomorrow will worry about itself."
Matthew 6:25-27, 33-34.

Along with the spirit of despair
Isaiah 61:3 (NIV).

and the spirit of falsehood,
1 John 4:6 (NIV).

"For God has not given us a spirit of fear, but of power and of love and of a sound mind*."*
2 Timothy 1:7 (NKJV, emphasis added).

The word worry comes from the old Anglo-Saxon verb wyrgan, *meaning "to choke or strangle,"*
Peale, *Enthusiasm Makes the Difference*, 73.

"Then the peace of God that exceeds all understanding . . . safe in Christ Jesus."
Philippians 4:6-7.

In God's Psychiatry, Charles Allen explains . . . ("treatment," "healing," or "restoring").
Charles L. Allen, *God's Psychiatry* (Grand Rapids: Baker, 1953), 7.

In other words, the healing of the mind . . . that God restored his soul
Psalm 23:3 (NIV 1984).

later in the Psalms, he wrote . . . wondrous acts from long ago.
Psalm 77:11.

"The longer the break . . . used to the feeling again."
Reardon, *Complete Idiot's Guide to Getting a Tattoo,* 175.

"When I started removing them, . . . that will deter them from getting (tattoos)."
www.aoltv.com/2011/02/08/mark-wahlberg-makes-kids-watch-tattoo-removal/.

Only instead of being expensive, it's a free gift of God;
Romans 6:23.

instead of requiring a few sessions, Jesus' sacrifice was final;
Hebrews 9:25-26.

instead of leaving any reminders of the old behind, . . . through him.
Hebrews 7:25.

God's grace is sufficient because God's power . . . rest on him.
2 Corinthians 12:9.

John Reardon writes, "Drawing . . . an art than a craft."
Reardon, *Complete Idiot's Guide to Getting a Tattoo,* 92.

And as we've seen, we are his masterpiece.
Ephesians 2:10 (NLT).

In the fall of 1991, Erika and Helmut Simon of Germany . . . into fine cuts in his skin.
www.iceman.it/en.

"Great thoughts reduced to practice become great acts."
William Hazlitt, *Table Talk Essays on Men and Manners* (London, 1821–1822).

Then determine to do what Paul the apostle did . . . what is ahead.
Philippians 3:13.

The psalmist wrote that he remembered the days, . . . handiwork.
Psalm 143:5.

Conclusion: Indelible

"some will say, 'I belong to the LORD' " . . . 'The LORD's.' "
Isaiah 44:5 (NIV).

"made by punctures rendered indelible . . . or with the name of Christ."
Clarke, *Clarke's Commentary on the Bible*, http://clarke.biblecommenter.com/isaiah/44.htm.

God calls to him to go throughout the city of Jerusalem . . . in the city.
Ezekiel 9:3-4.

Scholars believe this man is an Old Testament reference . . . occur there.
Matthew Henry's Whole Bible Commentary, http://biblecommenter.com/ezekiel/9-3.htm.

In Isaiah, God tells His people that He has inscribed . . . before Him.
Isaiah 49:16.

It's the same root word that is used in Proverbs . . . earth.
Proverbs 8:29.

"The idea is, that God had laid out the plan of Jerusalem . . . remembered them."
Barnes' Notes on the Bible, http://biblecommenter.com/isaiah/49-16.htm.

Of the A.D. 70 siege, the first-century Jewish historian Josephus . . . city.
Josephus Flavius, *The Wars of the Jews: History of the Destruction of Jerusalem*, bk. 6, chap. 1.8.

"Even if our bodies are breaking down on the outside, . . . every day."
2 Corinthians 4:16.

"Our temporary minor problems . . . things that can't be seen are eternal."
2 Corinthians 4:17-18.

"I have set before you . . . blessings and curses."
Deuteronomy 30:19 (NIV).

"bore our sins in his body on the tree, so that we might die to sins and live for righteousness."
1 Peter 2:24 (NIV 1984).

"who was and is and is coming"
Revelation 4:8.

He allows us to be active participants in our design, . . . image.
See 1 Corinthians 15:49.

And He has promised not to abandon the works of His hand.
Psalm 138:8.

Newberg said that even if we believe that the scriptures . . . God is.
Newberg and Waldman, *How God Changes Your Brain*, 241–48.

"God, your plans are . . . they outnumber grains of sand!"
Psalm 139:17-18.

First, unlike a dog to a man, God created us and we are made in God's image.
Genesis 1:27.

"I am the way, the truth, and the life. . . . Father."
John 14:6-7.

He is the Word that "became flesh and made his home among us" and we have seen his glory.
John 1:14.

"This is where the stakes are high and the mistakes are permanent."
Ink Master, Spike TV, 2011.

"the same yesterday, today and forever."
Hebrews 13:8.

"King of kings and Lord of lords."
Revelation 19:16.